COPYWRITING STRATEGIES

Copywriting Strategies

A No-Nonsense Guide to Writing Persuasive Copy for Your Business

Nicki Krawczyk

ROCKRIDGE
PRESS

For general information on our other products and services or to obtain technical support, please contact our Customer Care Department within the United States at (866) 744-2665, or outside the United States at (510) 253-0500.

Rockridge Press publishes its books in a variety of electronic and print formats. Some content that appears in print may not be available in electronic books, and vice versa.

Cover Designer: Lori Cervone
Interior Designer: Patricia Fabricant
Art Producer: Janice Ackerman
Editor: Mo Mozuch
Production Manager: Holly Haydash
Production Editor: Melissa Edeburn

Illustration used under license from Shutterstock.com.
Author photo courtesy of Jessie Wyman Photography.

Paperback ISBN: 978-1-63807-947-7 | eBook ISBN 978-1-63807-555-4
R0

To my dad, Mike Krawczyk,
who taught me how to write;
and to my mom, Pam Krawczyk,
who taught me how to
work for myself.

Contents

Introduction

I don't remember being paid for my first writing gig, but the career that followed certainly made up for that—and then some. When I was in high school (roughly eight billion years ago), my dad, who was a marketing director, would bring home writing work for me to do and then give me feedback. Again, I don't specifically remember being paid, though I must have been. Dad's very fair.

After that, my early 20s brought a disappointing run of jobs in public relations, special events, and health club management. Thanks to a gentle reminder from my mom (great parents, huh?), I rediscovered copywriting, made an abrupt pivot into a new career, and never looked back.

Now, nearly 20 years later, I've written copy for multi-billion-dollar brands like Hasbro, Tripadvisor, adidas, Keurig, and Marshalls; I've also written for solopreneurs and for businesses of just about every size. And for the last decade or so, my team and I have been teaching people to build professional copywriting careers of their own.

So, what does all this information mean for you? It means that I can teach you to write copy. Maybe not perfectly, but effectively enough to build your business and meet your goals until you're earning enough to hire a copywriter of your own.

But first, let's take a step back: What *is* copywriting? And why does knowing about copywriting matter? Simply put, copywriting is marketing and advertising writing. Copy—the words you write—is created to sell or persuade. Copywriting is about getting people to take action or, at the very least, to think a certain way about something.

Good copywriting means effective messaging, which is the basis for any successful business, organization, or enterprise. Period. You can have the prettiest graphics, the swankiest spokesperson, or the flashiest product, but without effective, insightful messaging, your efforts will fall apart.

This book is for you if you own or run a business and want to connect with your current and future customers in an efficient, effective, and, yes, genuine way.

In fact, copywriting is a powerful tool for anyone who needs to reach an audience. Nonprofits, this book is for you, too!

Anyone who loves writing and is curious about the field of copywriting will benefit from this book as well. Although it is by no means a resource sufficient to build an entire career on (show me any one book that is!), it is nevertheless a great one for dipping your toes in and learning more.

As you go through the chapters, you'll learn the foundational principles of writing copy, and you'll be challenged to put your new knowledge into action. Like any other endeavor, writing copy requires practice!

The exercises aren't just for their own sake, though. Oooooh no. These exercises will lay the foundation for your own effective messaging. They're the basis for the wildly effective copy and campaigns I've written for my clients, and they're the pillars of the wildly successful copywriting careers my students have built.

How to Use This Book

Y ou'll find the chapters of *Copywriting Strategies* grouped into three sections.

Part One: Copywriting 101 shares the elemental principles you'll need to know.

Part Two: Fundamental Copywriting Strategies teaches you how to put those principles into use. Each chapter of this section includes a "strategy session" with how-to information and some true-to-life examples of copywriting.

Part Three: Specific Copywriting Strategies builds on your new skills with advice on writing specific types of copy. Each of these chapters also provides a strategy session and true-to-life examples.

There are a couple of different ways to approach this book, depending on how you like to learn and what you need right now.

If you're the methodical type, and you like to absorb information in a structured sequence, just start at the beginning and work your way through to the end. You can do the exercises as you go or come back and work through them once you've finished reading.

Or, if you're on a more specific mission—as in, "I need to write this sales page . . . NOW"—you have another option. If you're going for speed and effectiveness or don't have the time or inclination to read from the beginning:

Start with chapter 1, where I'll go over some essential concepts you need to know.

Skip to chapter 3 and make friends with the 10 hard-and-fast rules of copywriting.

When you're done with the rules, read through the strategy sessions in chapters 4 to 10. (That sounds like a lot but isn't really.)

Then, look through chapters 16 to 22 to find the kind of copy you need to write right away and have a go! (This might sound a bit like those choose-your-own-adventure books from childhood: "Turn to page 9 to fight the witch, or turn to page 23 to save the prince." But what is marketing if not an adventure?)

We tend to forget when we become adults that learning something new takes time. And you won't master anything without practice. So as you work through the exercises in this book, don't beat yourself up when your first words aren't perfect. Nobody's are! Really, nobody's.

Also, be aware that you won't retain all of these concepts after you read them. You'll have to come back to the information here periodically for a refresher about, for example, just why you need to focus on the benefit (see page 27) and how to direct your audience to take action (see page 69).

So, work through this book in the way that's best for you. BUT be open to—dare I even say, "embrace"?—coming back to what you learn again and again to practice, hone, and master the skills that will serve you throughout your copywriting journey.

Ready? Let's dig in!

PART ONE

Copywriting 101

I know, you want to know *exactly* how to write the kinds of headlines, taglines, subject lines, or body copy that will have people clamoring to hire you, donate to you, or buy from you.

We'll get there, I promise! But if you start trying to write copy without understanding the foundational principles, you're setting yourself up for failure (or, at least, a very unpleasant experience). So, you need a good understanding of the basics of copywriting, including how copywriting has changed in the digital age. But before you can hit the ground running, let's bring you up to speed.

CHAPTER 1

UNDERSTANDING COPYWRITING

If you have some knowledge or experience with writing, set aside whatever you learned in seventh-grade English or Intro to Journalism (which is a relief, maybe?). Copywriting is vastly different from any other kind of writing. This chapter covers what makes copywriting different and why those differences are precisely what makes great copy connect with your audience and drive them to take action.

What Is Copywriting, Really?

Copywriting is marketing and advertising writing; in other words, text designed to sell or persuade. Copy is used to influence thinking and get people to take action.

But before you toss this book aside in frustration, moaning, "But I don't want to be salesy! I don't want to be manipulative or pushy!" I have good news for you.

Good copywriting is NOT about being salesy or pushy. By and large, "salesy and pushy" don't work in the long run and just leave people feeling kind of icky all over. Fundamentally, copywriting is about connecting an audience who has a *want* or *need* with the person, company, or organization that has the *solution* to that want or need.

We do that by crafting effective copy that makes the target audience say to themselves: "Wow, they get me . . . Hmm, this might be what I need . . . Hey! This is *exactly* what I need!"

Copy is the messaging used in banner ads, emails, websites, product packaging, direct mail, billboards, videos, TV and radio commercials, and sales webinars. Copy is the messaging on flashy online sales pages and on flyers posted on your local grocery store bulletin board. If you see messaging with the goal of persuasion or sales . . . it's copy.

So at a basic level, the messaging in any advertising is copywriting. But copywriting is so much more. It welcomes and nurtures your audience to build a relationship with your brand—without you having to interact person to person. Copywriting is how you share your story and make your message matter to the right people. And copywriting is how you offer solutions and opportunities.

A good copywriter understands that people don't buy products or services, they buy transformations like a life-saving medical treatment or four years of university tuition or improvements like a new T-shirt or a diet soda.

There is *no better predictor* of whether a venture will succeed or fail than the copy that supports the project. You can have the best product or service in the world and the prettiest photos, but if you can't communicate how great what you're selling is, you'll fail. Let's put a stake in the ground: Messaging is the single most important factor in the success of any business or endeavor.

Which makes you, as a copywriter, pretty dang important.

GOOD COPYWRITING . . .

- Is focused on the target audience and what they want and need to hear.

- Combines creativity and strategy.

- Makes a genuine connection with the target audience.

- Is well planned and well strategized.

- Uses the language of the target audience.

- Has clear objectives and meets them.

- Is simple to understand.

- Has a consistent brand voice.

- Leaves out the fluff and non-essentials.

- Catches the target audience's attention.

GOOD COPYWRITING IS NOT . . .

- Pushy or manipulative.

- Clever or funny for clever or funny's sake.

- About the copywriter.

- Even, really, about the company or organization being written for.

- Only used in marketing or advertising settings.

- Easy to write, necessarily . . . but is worth the effort.

- Always obvious . . . but is always effective.

Arguably, copywriting has been around as long as humans have been able to read and write and have had something to sell. If that definition's a little too broad, some put the advent of today's narrower meaning of copywriting as far back as the 1400s.

This book, though, examines modern copywriting and the tactics still in use today. Some ads of the past represent some standout moments; I encourage you to do some research and see for yourself what makes them great.

"They Laughed When I Sat Down at the Piano—But When I Started to Play!"

John Caple's 1926 ad is widely viewed as one of the first real breakout copywriting pieces. Created to drum up correspondence-course students for the U.S. School of Music, this advertisement was one of the first to reflect the motivation behind a purchase and the transformation a purchaser hopes for. The full ad is shockingly long by today's standards but is also a testament to how a compelling story and an inspiring transformation can drive people to read an ad and then take action.

Volkswagen Beetle Ads from the 1960s

Even five decades later, this copy-led campaign for the brand-new Beetle remains one of the most interesting and creative you'll ever come across. The Doyle Dane Burnbach company was tasked with introducing an unconventional car to the market and devised an unconventional method to do so by adopting an irreverent and starkly honest tone. Embracing the vehicle's small size and comparatively low price, DDB wrote headlines like "It Makes Your House Look Bigger" and "Live Below Your Means." Though not a perfect campaign with plenty of product-of-the-time, cringe-worthy elements ("Women are soft and gentle, but they hit things"), the ad series is nonetheless fascinating for its ability to capitalize on a counterculture, antiestablishment, truth-telling movement of the day and use those aspects . . . to sell cars.

⟶

"Got Milk?" and "Just Do It"

Launched in 1988 and 1993, respectively, these two taglines are both effective pieces of copy and cultural markers for the late 20th century (and beyond). As any copywriter will tell you, distilling a brand down to just a few words—and then making those words stick with their target audience—is one of the hardest jobs you can do. Nike created both a brand aesthetic and a rallying cry with "Just Do It," inspiring people to take on the mantle of the athlete with each purchase. "Got Milk?" took the interesting tactic of not overtly trying to get people to purchase the product, focusing instead on the inevitability of wanting and needing it, saying, in effect, "You already know you need milk. Do you have some, or do you need to hit the grocery store?" The ad represents a fascinating twist and manages to accomplish that pivot with just two little words.

Facebook Ads

In 2007, Facebook launched an ad platform and in so doing suddenly made connecting with millions of members of a target audience possible for virtually any business, anytime, anywhere. Never before could small business play in the same league as bigger competitors—*and* get access to the same advanced targeting and analytics.

Common Misconceptions about Copywriting

Copywriting has nothing to do with the legal action of "copyrighting" nor, for that matter, "copy editing." You may occasionally come across misunderstandings about these terms and need to correct them. More important, though, are the misconceptions outlined over the next few pages, that run rampant among people who don't understand copywriting. And if you buy into these misconceptions, they may get in the way of you doing your best work.

MISCONCEPTION: COPYWRITING MUST BE ENTERTAINING

The truth: Copywriting isn't about entertainment; it's about communication. Sure, a copywriter may sometimes use a story or humor to make a point. But the end goal must be *making that point*. Copywriting needs to catch a reader's attention, but the most effective way to do so is by communicating what matters to the reader. Entertainment is secondary, if even an element at all.

MISCONCEPTION: THE BEST COPYWRITING IS THE FUNNIEST COPYWRITING

The truth: Similar to our previous point, some copywriting may be funny, but humor is not essential—and is never going to be the primary purpose of a line of copy. Think about it: Most businesses have no need for funny copy. Banks, tech firms, clothing brands, grocery stores, health coaches, nonprofits, and thousands of other industries don't need humor in their messaging. If being funny is within a brand's style *and* enhances the effectiveness of the message then, great, humor is useful. Otherwise, it has no place in the copy.

MISCONCEPTION: COPYWRITING ISN'T "REAL" WRITING

The truth: I've found that you're most likely to hear this one from struggling novelists or poets; successful novelists or poets don't take any issue with copywriting. Copywriting involves wielding words to convey a message and is just as much "real" writing as any other type. And I'm certain that F. Scott Fitzgerald, Kurt Vonnegut, and James Patterson, who were all copywriters before they were novelists, would agree.

MISCONCEPTION: COPYWRITING IS ONLY HIP TAGLINES AND SLOGANS

The truth: Many people who think of copywriters imagine a cool young writer in some hot downtown ad agency working for months to come up with a single great line to encapsulate a brand. (Matthew McConaughey in the film *How to Lose a Guy in 10 Days* and the horrendously bad "Frost Yourself" slogan come to mind.) Yes, copywriting can involve writing taglines or slogans to encapsulate a brand or campaign but there's so much more—emails, websites, direct mail, billboards, packaging; the to-do list for a copywriter goes on and on.

MISCONCEPTION: TEMPLATES OR AI SOFTWARE CAN REPLACE COPYWRITING

The truth: More effort than ever is being put into developing artificial intelligence programs that can write copy. But even a sophisticated AI bot can't be creative—can't come up with possibilities that *make sense* and that no one's ever heard before. It just can't. The very nature of an AI program is to be derivative and work from preexisting ideas. And an AI bot certainly can't come up with a new concept on the fly when someone needs a quick change. Similarly, templates ("Just plug in a few keywords and you've got a perfect sales email!") have severe limitations. Effective copywriting is about custom-crafting a message based on the unique combination of an audience, a purpose for the message, a benefit for the audience, and an action for them to take. No premade, broad-strokes template is going to be able to accomplish what the copywriter can.

The Difference between Copywriting and Other Kinds of Writing

The biggest point of confusion for many would-be copywriters is the difference between copywriting and content writing. (If you're considering hiring a copywriter who doesn't know the difference, you should definitely reconsider.) Copywriting, as I'll persist in hammering home, is writing designed to sell or persuade. Content writing, on the other hand, is writing designed to educate, entertain, or inspire (or any combination of the three).

Content writing includes blog posts, articles, video scripts. A blog post about how to make the perfect hollandaise sauce; a quiz helping you identify which '80s sitcom character you are most like; a listicle (content presented in list form) about the top hotel pools in Positano—all are examples of content writing.

Broadly speaking, you could even put novels, screenplays, plays, short stories, and other types of creative writing in the "content" category. Their primary purpose, usually, is to entertain, sometimes with a bit of education thrown in for good measure. This very book? A prime example of content.

Content writing can be part of a company's interactions with potential customers and can be used to nurture a target reader, maintain an audience's attention, and encourage the reader to like and trust a brand. Content can educate people about products, teach them how to use products, and even just keep them on a website to help that website generate ad revenue.

Copywriting, though, has a different purpose and needs to be approached differently. I view copywriting as similar to a word puzzle—you have an objective to meet (a puzzle to solve) and certain elements you can combine in a variety of ways to meet that objective. Copywriting makes for a fascinating and fun marriage of strategy and creativity.

Why Doing Your Own Copywriting (at Least at First) Is Important

As someone who trains professional copywriters, I'm never going to tell you that writing your own copy is always the best solution. Unless you choose to dedicate yourself to writing copy, you're not going to achieve the mastery a professional copywriter attains.

Which makes sense, right? You might be able to DIY a leak in your kitchen, but you know you're no professional plumber (or if you are, let's switch that metaphor to changing the oil in your car and not being a mechanic).

That said, writing your own copy at first will benefit you a great deal. Now that you're learning the principles of what makes effective copy, viewing your own message through this lens is incredibly valuable.

Many business owners never take the time to ask themselves the questions a copy project requires them to ask: "What does my target audience get out of this?" or "How does this meet my target's desire?" And because these business owners never ask these questions, they never discover the key drivers that make their products or services compelling to their would-be customers.

Even if you intend to hire copywriters—as, quite frankly, you should when you have the resources—the experience of having written your own copy will empower you to work better with them when the time comes. You'll be more equipped to evaluate the work they do and contribute insights to make the copy the best possible.

Becoming competent at copywriting will give you an enhanced understanding of how to make your business compelling for your audience. This skill will only improve your business performance not to mention your personal communication. And when you're ready, your copywriting knowledge will help you hire the right copywriter to take you to the next level.

CHAPTER 2

COPYWRITING IN THE DIGITAL AGE

O kay, not exactly a news flash, but the advent of the internet *did* change a few things for a few people—copywriters among them. This chapter takes you through what's changed and, of course, how you can take full advantage in the copy you write.

Copywriting and the World Wide Web

There was a time, not that long ago, when if you wanted to reach your target audience, you had to figure out which magazines or newspapers you thought they might read and then advertise there, hoping they'd notice. Or you had to buy a list of names and addresses and send your message to them through the mail. Or you had to put up big signs along the road. These were pretty much your only advertising choices.

Today marketers have increasingly more sophisticated ways to reach their exact target audiences. At the same time, though, they face increasingly more competition for those coveted eyeballs. Combine these circumstances with short attention spans, the proliferation of new media platforms, and the ability to consume digital media from our computers, tablets, phones, and even watches, and you have a pretty amazing but challenging opportunity.

Hootsuite reported that as of January 2021, the average amount of time spent online each day per person was 6 hours and 54 minutes. As you might expect, this number has increased over time. EMarketer reported that 2019 was the first year digital advertising hit more than 50 percent of all advertising dollars spent and predicted the number to rise to almost 68 percent by 2024. People are spending more and more time online, and the smartest advertisers and marketers are ensuring that they reach people there. So let's talk about what you, as a copywriter, need to know—and how you can take advantage of these trends.

HOW THE INTERNET HAS IMPACTED COPYWRITING

When you take a step back and really think about it, the internet is, in fact, pretty magical. At any moment, from practically anywhere on the planet, you can call up any kind of information, communication, or entertainment you choose. Amazing for consumers but a pretty big challenge for marketers and copywriters. Here's why.

WE'RE MORE DISTRACTIBLE THAN EVER.
On the upside, if people are distractible you can lure them away from what they were previously doing with your great copy. On the downside, they can be lured away from *you* if you fail to keep them interested. And because many people are interacting with multiple screens at the same time, you're not just up against the distractions from one device, you're up against distractions from all of them.

COMPARING OPTIONS IS EASY.
Imagine you own the only grocery store in town. Odds are pretty good that most people are going to shop at your store, right? You just have to stay stocked with the products people want, and they'll buy. But now imagine that a dozen other grocery stores move onto your same block. And what's more, they all display their prices in

the windows so that all people have to do is stroll by to compare. Welcome to the internet. People can easily compare all possible options for any purchase decision they need to make. Offering something to purchase is not enough; you need to communicate exactly why you're the best choice.

INSTANT GRATIFICATION HAS DECREASED OUR PATIENCE.
A few years ago, people were willing to dig around a bit on your website to figure out who you are and what you do. Wave goodbye to that luxury. Today's consumers have no patience for messaging that's vague or at all unclear. They expect to find exactly what they want, immediately, and exactly where they expect to. So, you have to be both purposeful in your messaging and purposeful in where you put that messaging.

WE CAN PURCHASE ALMOST ANYTHING, INSTANTLY.
Isn't this good news for business owners? Well, being able to purchase instantly should be . . . but because people are making up their minds about products and services faster than ever, winning over potential customers who typically go elsewhere can be a challenge.

THERE IS NO "DOWNTIME."
People expect brands to be available at all times and they also expect responses to requests (and news) instantly. And for a brand that wants to build a relationship with its audience, managing all the messages that need to go out and keeping them timely can be hard.

HOW SOCIAL MEDIA HAS IMPACTED COPYWRITING

For a long time, advertising was not a game most business owners could afford to play. Generally speaking, only the big, well-funded brands could advertise on TV, radio, or in high-distribution magazines or newspapers. Smaller local companies were relegated to advertising in local papers and in local TV ad slots, if they could even afford to shoulder these costs. Advertising in big markets started in the thousands of dollars, which meant most businesses—and certainly most self-funded entrepreneurs—could never afford to give large-scale, large-audience advertising a shot.

Then came social media. Or, more specifically, then came social media advertising. Platforms like Facebook and Instagram suddenly made widespread advertising accessible to everyone. Starting at just a few dollars a day, almost any brand could get their message in front of their perfect potential purchasers.

And because now almost anyone can advertise, seemingly almost everyone does. The competition on social media platforms has ramped up as advertisers work to attract attention away from both regular content *and* other advertisers.

A brand that wants to keep up must move fast and iterate wisely. Traditional advertising used to take weeks (or even months) to develop a new campaign and ads. With social media, that time line is now days—if not hours. The challenge for social media advertisers is to keep the messaging perpetually fresh, interesting, and relevant to the audience.

The good news from the advertiser's perspective is that where traditional advertising used to mean waiting weeks or months before knowing if a (very expensive) ad campaign had any kind of effect, with social media tracking, the advertiser can know within days. Even better, they can quickly and easily test ads to see which have more impact on which audiences.

So instead of rolling the dice on one big, expensive TV spot, social media advertisers can test multiple messages to multiple audiences in multiple placements. Does this make everything a bit complicated? Sure. But this situation can also make copywriting even more fun.

DEALING WITH DATA

Don't skip this section! I know the word "data" probably made your eyes glaze over. But here's a secret: A data set is a copywriter's best friend.

The truth is, no matter how skilled a copywriter you are, you can't know *for sure* if your messaging is going to resonate with an audience before you put what you've written out into the world. Sure, you can do focus groups, poll people, phone a friend—but there's just no way to know how your copywriting is actually going to perform.

Which is why you need to learn to love data. All of the digits and percentage points on your advertising platforms or in your email software give you concrete feedback about what's working and what's not. Once you understand what you're looking at and what you're looking for, you can use that data to make smart decisions and vastly improve your results.

I could easily write a whole book on data and testing, so we can't possibly cover this entire topic right here. That said, I've spelled out three important data points (aka three "metrics") to keep your eye on. Get to know the concepts behind these metrics. In part 2 of this book, you'll learn how to acquire the skills to improve your numbers.

Open Rate—the percentage of people that opens the emails you send to them. You'll find this statistic provided by your email software. Why are open rates important? Well, if people aren't opening your emails, they'll never see what's in the body of your message! Benchmarks vary pretty wildly between industries but 15 to 25 percent should be what you shoot for initially. Once you hit your goal, try testing out new subject lines to see how your audience responds.

Click-Through Rate—the percentage of people who click on the link you've provided. This link could be in an ad or email or on a webpage. The click-through rate tells you how compelling the messaging is. The more persuasive the copy, the more people click that link, creating a higher click-through rate. Always test

$\longrightarrow$

the messaging that accompanies your links to see what gets your audience to take action.

Conversion Rate—the percentage of people who are "converted" from one state to another, depending on the action you want them to take. People may go from non–email subscribers to subscribers, for example, or from non-purchasers to purchasers. These rates are important to track regularly to ensure they're always trending upward or at least staying roughly the same. New messaging on your sales page that takes your conversion rate from 4 to 6 percent may not sound like a big deal, but this difference could represent hundreds of thousands of dollars in additional revenue for a business. (So yeah, copywriting is a pretty big deal, huh?)

Types of Digital Copywriting

By and large, digital copywriting is going to be "direct-response copywriting," meaning copy that's intended to make people take an immediate action.

Brand copywriting—the other side of the copy coin—is more about creating general awareness of and setting a tone for a brand. Frankly, branding is (mostly, in the simplest terms) a luxury that big-money advertisers can afford and that most of us cannot. I suggest you stay focused on direct response for your business or company until you're pulling in, oh, let's say a few hundred million a year in revenue.

We'll talk about the different types of digital copywriting over the next few pages, but before we do I'd like you to be aware of a few points. First, I won't give you an exhaustive list, just some of the biggest categories. New messaging opportunities are popping up all the time (video! chatbots! SMS texting!), so listing them all is impossible. But I'll cover the best messaging venues for you to start with and focus on as you build your messaging plan.

Second, know that whereas these are all different types of messaging, *they all follow the copywriting principles laid out in the rest of this book.* Where you place the copy, or how much copy you're able to use, will vary. But the way you strategize that copy and decide what messages to get across will not. Master the foundations, hone your skills, and you can wield them anywhere you need to communicate.

EMAIL COPY

Email is still one of the most effective means of communicating with your target audience. After all—because we are not talking about spam—they opted in! The people you're contacting *want* to hear from you!

HOW YOU'LL USE EMAIL COPY

Email is great for notifying people about pop-up sales and new inventory but is also incredibly useful for nurturing your audience and increasing the degree to which they like and trust you. So be sure to always stay focused on messaging that is useful or valuable to your subscribers. But experiment with what you send. Share your origin story or customer success stories, bust myths, overcome your target's objections, answer frequently asked questions—the options and opportunities are bountiful.

As you get more advanced in your marketing and copywriting, you can start experimenting with email funnels. In a nutshell, an email funnel is an automated series of emails that takes subscribers from one state to another. People may go, then, from "newly aware of your brand" to "purchaser" through a sequence of carefully strategized emailed messages that get them increasingly familiar with your brand, educate them on what makes your product superior, and then excite them enough to purchase.

WEBSITE COPY

Sure, website copy refers to your home page and "About Us" page, but the copy on your landing page, sales page, and services page is included here, too. And don't forget about the copy on those sneaky, easy-to-forget pages—like the one people see after they've opted in to your emails.

HOW YOU'LL USE WEBSITE COPY

The key to effective website copy is to be aware of the customer journey: how and when a typical customer navigates to each page on your site.

For example, in the case of a landing page from an ad, people may click there with no other knowledge about you other than what they read in the advertisement. What do you need to convey on that landing page, then, to get them to take the action you want them to take?

With a "Services" page, the likelihood is high that someone has navigated there because they specifically want to know what services you offer. I know what I'm saying sounds obvious but think about what this information tells you. These customers are already somewhat interested in purchasing from you. They have enough base-level trust in your brand to want to learn more about what you offer. That still puts them on a pretty wide spectrum between "casually interested" and "ready to buy" but comes with a lot of information about what additional messages could be helpful to the reader on that page.

BANNER OR SOCIAL AD COPY

The copy on banner ads is some of the toughest you'll have to write because here you'll need to convey a lot in very, very few words. Social ad copy may allow for more words than a website banner, but you're still facing the same fundamental challenge: Advertising is about interrupting someone and getting them to redirect their attention to you.

Imagine: There's your target audience member scrolling down a website or looking through their social feed. And here's you, the advertiser, inserting your ad, trying to catch their eye and get them to stop scrolling, read your ad, and click. You're actually making a pretty big ask: "Stop whatever you're doing and start doing something totally different." And yet, if you know what you're doing as a copywriter, you can succeed.

HOW YOU'LL USE BANNER OR SOCIAL AD COPY

Before you even think about advertising, make sure you know and understand your target audience inside and out. (We'll talk about how to identify your target audience in part 2; see page 36.) You can't possibly craft a message that will get their attention if you don't understand what they think and what they want.

But when you've mastered accurately reading your audience, you'll have a wildly effective tool to generate visits ("traffic") to your website or to specific pages you want people to visit (or both). Need to increase your email list? Run an ad campaign on a website your audience likes, which directs them to your compelling opt-in page. Want to turn visitors into customers? Run a re-targeting campaign that reaches people who have visited your content (and are now familiar with you) and that sends them to your product pages so they can purchase! The possibilities are vast, and we're only scratching the surface.

OPT-IN COPY

For any kind of business or organization—profit or nonprofit, from a multi-billion-dollar global enterprise down to a one-person business—having an email list will be a major factor for success. And the major factor in the success of the email list? The opt-in copy; that is, the copy that invites people to receive the business's or organization's emails.

All you're asking people for is their email address, right? Easy! Except that asking people to take any kind of action requires strategy. If there isn't a clear and compelling benefit to them for giving you their email address . . . they just won't do it. Why would they? For every website that says something bland and ineffectual like "Sign up for our newsletter," there's a copywriter sadly shaking their head.

First, let's talk about the "what"—what are people going to get for signing up? A discount? A freebie? A useful resource? And no, "news about us" or "being the first to know" isn't enough. If you want people's email addresses, you have to give them something they want in return.

And then comes "where." Where will you place this copy? *Everywhere*. You want to make opting in to your list easy for people to do anytime they want. So many websites display an opt-in pop-up right away but give visitors no other place to opt in. What about the people who closed that pop-up because they didn't yet care enough about the brand, but they wanted to opt in later? Don't make people hunt to find your opt-in box; most just won't make the effort.

PRODUCT DESCRIPTION COPY

Oh, the missed opportunities! Product description copy is, as you might have guessed, the short paragraph that describes an item, often with ideas for where and how to use it. Now that you're aware of product description, I challenge you to start reading this kind of copy critically whenever you see it. Notice how often you find lazy copy like "goes with any outfit" or "looks great with any décor."

HOW YOU'LL USE PRODUCT DESCRIPTION COPY
A good product description should do double duty. The copy should not only literally describe the product but draw attention to any elements not obvious from the product photos or illustrations.

When you write a product description, consider where the reader is in the customer journey. If they've gotten to the point of reading about the product, they are very close to making the decision about whether to purchase. So think carefully about what information you can give them to tilt their decision in your favor.

What makes this product better than other options? Or unique? How, where, and when would they use this product? What are they missing out on if they *don't* buy what you're selling?

SEARCH ENGINE OPTIMIZATION (SEO) COPY

Ready for a little secret? There's no such thing as search engine optimization copywriting.

Sure, there's definitely such a thing as search engine optimization (SEO). In essence, SEO involves a series of tactics designed to increase the chances that a webpage will rank higher on a search engine results page when someone searches for terms that pertain to that business or organization. For example, if you own a store that sells glow-in-the-dark dog clothing, when people search "glow-in-the-dark Chihuahua sweaters" you really want your website to appear as one of the first search results. SEO is the practice of (helping to) making that happen.

One of the tactics for optimizing your website for search engines is to use important keywords to allow search engines to find them. But here's the thing: A good copywriter, writing well-strategized copy, should be naturally using those terms in their copy because these are the terms that describe and define the product or service. If you sell glow-in-the-dark Chihuahua sweaters and *don't* use those words, well, your messaging might need a bit more work.

Truth is, there just won't be enough copy on your website to pack in enough search terms to make a substantive difference. So where *does* SEO matter? In content writing. In copy, you might be able to use the term "glow-in-the-dark Chihuahua sweaters" within a headline on a product page. But if you really want to have an impact on your SEO, you'd be better served writing a piece of useful content about glow-in-the-dark Chihuahua sweaters, where you can use the term several times, provide other information, and use other keywords that searchers (and search engines) deem valuable.

This description is a vast oversimplification of the increasingly complicated field of SEO. But what's important is to get clear about what copy can and cannot do. If you're looking to boost the (long-term) impact of search engine optimization for your website, you're not looking for copywriting, you're looking for content. Undoubtedly this statement will ruffle a few feathers, but I'll say it again: "SEO copywriting" does not actually exist.

SOCIAL MEDIA CAPTIONS

Remember when we talked about how copy is designed to sell or persuade and content is designed to inspire, educate, or entertain (see page 9)? Well, social media captions walk the line between the two.

Social media captions are the words that provide context or add additional info to an image or video that's shared on a social media account. Most captions are content; they tell stories, teach, share information. But some captions are copy: They ask the reader to take some sort of action. How can you tell which one you should write? You go into the situation with a plan.

HOW YOU'LL USE SOCIAL MEDIA CAPTIONS

The secret to the best social media accounts is that they are all well planned and strategized, sometimes weeks in advance. Even the most carefree posts that seem casually dropped into a feed have usually been planned, written, and approved ahead of time. And because you're smart, you'll do the same thing.

Sit down and plan the posts you'll put on your social media feed, and then plan what the captions will be. Yes, you can and should periodically ask people to take an action like commenting, sharing, or DMing you. But you also shouldn't make such requests all the time; you'll burn people out. The majority of your captions should be content that supports or enhances the image or video. Sometimes this includes a call to action ("Click the link in bio for more info!") and, yes, you have, in fact, spotted a gray area between copy and content. What's important to focus on is knowing the purpose of your caption and creating compelling writing.

When you use copy in your social media captions, do so sparingly and intelligently. For example, don't ask people to share a post just for the sake of sharing, ask them to share a post to enter into a sweepstakes. Remember that every action you ask people to take needs to benefit them in some way, otherwise they won't act. And when you choose to ask people to take action, the purpose for doing so should be strategic and one that supports your overall marketing plan.

WHERE DO I BEGIN?

Phew! Great question! There's a lot of opportunity and a lot you can do. Because I don't know you and I don't know your business or situation, I can't give you a perfect prescription for what copywriting projects to take on and in what order. But I *can* give you some guidelines for how to figure these points out for yourself.

One word of warning, though: Approach one project at a time. Digging into copywriting and refining your message can get overwhelming, especially at first. All of the potential mistakes and opportunities are suddenly glaring and seem to require your instant attention. Follow the steps below to create a plan for dealing with all of them in ways most beneficial for your business, nonprofit, or project.

Take inventory of all your messaging. Keep everything simple: Make a list of the places where you have—or need—copy. Be specific. Don't put "website" on your list; list all the individual pages. You can also include future projects.

Figure out what gets the most traffic or attention. Here's your chance to work with the data we mentioned earlier. What pieces of your messaging are people seeing most? Which social channels have the biggest following? Which pages on your website get the most visitors? Which types of email are recipients

$\longrightarrow$

most likely to open? Improvements to the most highly read messages have the biggest potential gain.

Evaluate your goals. First, evaluate your business, organization, or project as a whole. What goals are you working toward? More revenue? More repeat customers? Next, evaluate which copy projects would have the most impact on those goals.

Prioritize your projects accordingly. Clear winners will be projects that both have a high impact *and* already get a lot of traffic. After that, you'll have to evaluate where your opportunities lie. Don't forget to consider the potential of projects, too. Are there pieces of messaging that get a lot of eyes now that could be tweaked to have a bigger impact on the business?

Keep in mind, your plan of attack doesn't have to be perfect. This is just a set of guidelines to help you get started. As you dig in (and continue to learn and hone your copywriting skills), you'll uncover all kinds of new ideas and opportunities.

CHAPTER 3

10 HARD-AND-FAST RULES FOR COPYWRITING GREATNESS

No career could be fully encapsulated in a single book. But what this book *can* do is give you the most important guiding principles. The following 10 commandments of copywriting will steer you in the right direction, no matter what type of copy you're writing or medium you're writing for.

We'll dig deeper into each of these rules in the upcoming chapters—with examples of how they're used and advice for using them. But this quick list should serve as a good introduction as well as a handy reference whenever you need a refresher.

Sometimes copywriting involves rule-breaking; on any given job, many of the grammatical and structural rules our English teachers and professors taught us get tossed right out the window. But these 10 rules you'll want to learn by heart and come back to again and again.

They're not a magic formula for effective copy, but they're awfully close.

#1: Have a Purpose and Plan

You'd be surprised by the number of people who sit down to write copy without first thinking through *why* they're writing (aside from "I need an email") or what result they'd like to get.

SO BEFORE YOU START WRITING ANY PROJECT, ASK YOURSELF:

- What is the purpose of this project?
- What am I trying to accomplish?
- What do I want my audience to do; what action do I want them to take?

The answers form your strategy for the project. Create a document and write them at the top of the page so you don't forget what they are.

THEN FOLLOW UP WITH:

- What's the main benefit for my readers if they take this action?
- What does the target get out of doing this action?
- What message or information does my audience need to receive to want to take this action?

AND FINALLY:

- What's the clearest way I can ask them to take the action I want them to take?

Those answers form an outline to follow when you write. They don't have to be "copywritten" yet; at this stage, they're just notes. In a very simplified format, this means your messaging hierarchy will be:

- Benefit to reader
- Additional information that supports that benefit
- Call to action

Start with this and you're already halfway to success.

#2: It's Not about You

This can be hard for some business owners, marketers, or even copywriters to hear. But the truth is, the messaging you put out into the world is not about you. It's about your target audience and what they want or need to hear.

Many people make the mistake of focusing on what they want to tell people versus thinking through what their target audience actually cares about. For example, a marketing executive might get really excited about the voice-activated doors in a minivan and want to talk all about the new technology the company used to make that happen.

But the technology is not what their target audience cares about. Parents care that voice-activated doors mean that they don't have to decide between putting their grocery bag on the ground and watching the contents spill or putting a child down and risking them running into traffic.

So when you're putting together your messaging plan, think carefully about your target audience and put yourself in their shoes. What really matters to this audience? And how can you make your message more focused on them and what they want and need?

#3: Focus on the Benefit

If there *were* a silver bullet for copywriting success, it would be this: Focus your message on the benefit to consumers. Make crystal clear what they get out of what you want them to do. Or, in marketing parlance, be sure to let them know what's in it for them.

We have a whole chapter coming up on identifying the benefit so I won't get detailed here. But always remember: If you stay focused on the *benefit that matters to your target audience*, going wrong in your messaging is very hard to do.

The benefit answers the question in your reader's mind: "Why should I do this?" For example, your subject line answers the question "Why should I open this email?" Your headline answers the question "What's in it for me if I keep reading—and if I take the action they want me to take?" Your Facebook ad copy answers the question "What do I get out of clicking on this ad?"

This focus on the benefit isn't just effective in copywriting, by the way. Any time you want something from someone, focus on the benefit to them of doing what you'd like them to do. For example, if you want Jaye in accounting to forward you a report, focus on how that'll save *them* time later. This strategy isn't manipulation; it's effective communication. And it works.

#4: Be Attention-Grabbing

You've only got a few seconds to catch someone's attention before—poof!—they're gone. So your first line of any piece of copy needs to interest them enough to make them stop in their tracks.

Now, of course you can't be attention-grabbing just for attention's sake. Writing something shocking or scandalous unrelated to your message may catch a reader's attention but won't keep their focus for long and will likely only annoy them. This is the problem with "clickbait"—copy that interests people enough to click through but doesn't offer a pay off through appropriate information.

We'll talk about this more in chapter 7 (see page 54), but the key takeaway is to start your copy with something that genuinely interests your audience and is directly related to your overall message. Sometimes you'll create a great, benefit-heavy headline on a landing page and at other times, an intriguing statement at the beginning of a Facebook ad.

Either way, the key is to know your target audience and serve them up copy they can't ignore.

#5: Hold Attention

Getting your readers' initial attention isn't the only thing that counts! If they read only a bit of your copy and then leave, you haven't accomplished your goals.

Every piece of copy in your message—and every word in each piece of copy—has to serve a purpose. I realize this sounds like a lofty goal, but the moment your copy starts to veer from the main message—what's beneficial and valuable to your reader—is the exact moment you start losing their attention.

As you're going through your copy—first writing, then editing—continually ask yourself: Is this something they need to know? And, if so, is this something they need to know right here and right now? The more you keep your copy focused on the reader, the more you keep your audience's attention all the way through to your call to action.

#6: Use Words the Audience Uses

Good news: Using the same language your target audience uses is not cheating; it's a smart idea. When you use the same words and phrases as your audience to refer to the challenges, needs, wants, and hopes they face, they feel like you truly understand them.

Not sure what words they use? Find out! Get on a call with people who have purchased from you or who haven't purchased from you yet but represent your perfect audience. Ask about any frustrations they experience related to your product, service, or industry. Find out what success and happiness would look like for them if those issues were magically solved. Be brave and ask them what they like best and what they like least about what you have to offer.

Take notes, of course, but also record these calls—you're going to want to listen to them multiple times. And as you come across words your audience uses, make sure to use them later in your copy. This tactic makes your entire audience feel seen, heard, and understood.

#7: Don't Waste Words

In copywriting, every word counts—but that doesn't mean you get bonus points for additional words. No one is going to read everything you write, as much as it pains me to say so. Still, this is reality. *You'll* read all of your copy, your mother will, and perhaps your spouse will . . . but they're the only ones.

The challenge is to get your target audience to read as much of your copy as possible. A few key tactics come in handy in this regard.

First, be ruthless with streamlining your message. Have very high standards about what gets to stay and what has to go. Evaluate every paragraph, every sentence, every line, and, yes, every single word to make sure they are essential to your core message. If not? Gone.

One of the best ways to ensure people read copy is to keep your message focused . . . and brief. No one wants to read long paragraphs in any writing. And when it comes to copy, very few people will.

Keep your paragraphs short. Keep your sentences short. Keep your word choices simple. Cut anything that's just taking up space.

#8: Be Consistent

Your "brand voice" is your brand's personality and how that personality comes across. The voice might be friendly, straightforward, quirky, serious, or any combination of any number of traits. But when you use your brand voice, you need to make sure that you stay consistent throughout your project and across all of your copywriting.

Similarly, you want to stick to the style choices you make. Do your headlines capitalize each word (This Is A Headline)? Do they only capitalize the important words (This Is a Headline)? Or do they capitalize only the first word (This is a headline)? Pick one format to follow across all your copy.

Consistency may seem like nitpicking, but inconsistency is very jarring for the reader and can even erode trust. When your audience has trouble getting a clear sense of who you are as a brand, they have a hard time believing you'll deliver on the promises you make. And no one buys from a brand they don't trust.

Always track your voice, style, and word choices, and make sure to stick to them.

#9: Use a Single Call to Action

When a person comes to a fork in the road, they can only go one way—not both at once. Your reader is exactly the same. When they come to the end of your copy, they can only take one single action next, which is why giving them one main next step is important.

We call this next step the "call to action," and what's involved doesn't have to be complicated. Think: "Sign Up Here," "Download the Free Ebook," or "Buy Now." This process should be simple, and your readers should know exactly what will happen after they take that action.

Because each project you write has a single, main purpose (and they do, right? Go back to rule number one on page 26!), each should also have a single, main call to action.

#10: Copywriting Is Not Done When You're Done Writing

I'll be honest: You're not going to like this. No one does. You'll work hard on your copy, trying to get just the right message with just the right words. And you'll reach the end, sigh with relief, put down your pen or lift your fingers from the keyboard . . .

And you'll only be halfway done. The fact is, you should put just as much effort into *editing* your work as you do into initially *writing* it. No writer gets everything perfect the first time through, and you're not going to be the exception to that rule. (Sorry.)

But, at the same time, isn't knowing that you don't *have* to get everything perfect a relief?

Once you're done with your first draft, get up and walk away. Let your brain focus on something else for a while. If you have the time, give yourself a day or two before coming back to your copy.

Then, when you do, evaluate what you've written as objectively as possible. Review the list of rules in the box to see what needs to be strengthened, cut, clarified, and rearranged. Your first draft is important, but the editing and refining is what really makes your copy effective.

The more you use these rules, the more they'll become automatic elements of your copywriting. But even copywriting pros know that forgetting the fundamentals is pretty easy to do.

Because all of these rules will factor into each project you write, refer back to this list regularly. If there's anything you're going to photocopy and put up on your wall, this list of rules would be it.

First, use the 10-rules list (see pages 26 to 32) as a refresher before you start writing. Prime your brain with the key points you want to include and remember as you work.

Then, after you've finished your first draft, use the list as a checklist. This great resource can guide which edits need to be made and where.

And **finally,** if you're a copywriter working with a client, this list will serve a third purpose. Refer to the rules to evaluate feedback from your client and make sure any changes you make won't compromise the integrity and effectiveness of the project.

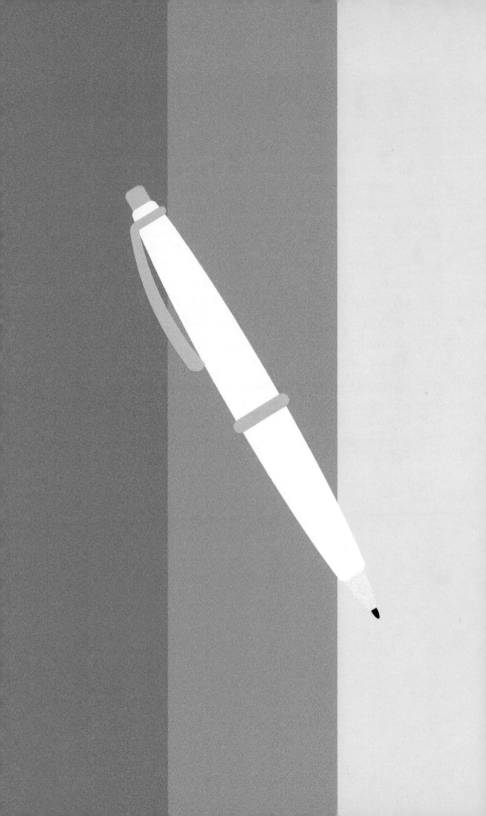

PART TWO

Fundamental Copywriting Strategies

Until now, we've talked in broad strokes about copywriting and shared some rules to write by. The time to dig in and start putting these principles into practice has arrived. This part covers the fundamentals inside and out by putting them to use.

CHAPTER 4

DEFINE YOUR AUDIENCE

Writing any message when you don't know who you're writing to is hard. And with copywriting, doing so is virtually impossible. You should always go into a project knowing what message you want to get across, but the message alone is not enough; if you don't know who you're writing to, you can't craft that message in a way that resonates with the reader.

Some business owners want to define their audience as "everyone." As in, they'll happily take sales from anybody who wants to buy. But in practical terms, an audience is never truly "everyone" or "anyone." Let's look at a clothing store, for example. Sure, anyone could purchase from there. But the largest group of purchasers at this particular store might be women ages 30 to 45 with a preppy style and a preference for value over brand names.

Trying to write for "everyone" instead of gearing your message to your true target audience ensures that the message ends up too broad and too vague to be effective.

This chapter helps you define your audience so you can write copy that will connect with them. And if you think you already know your target audience, I still encourage you to go through the following pages. You might just discover a few surprises.

Strategy Session

To start defining your audience, you're going to gather as much information about them as you can. To do this, look at the data you already have about your purchasers, look at the data about your subscribers, and look at the data about your social media followers.

If you have some trouble getting deeper data, ask your purchasers, subscribers, or followers to complete a survey. Not all of them will take the time to do so, but the information you get will still be very valuable. To entice more people to participate, you might want to add an incentive: a small discount, some sort of freebie, or an entrance into a giveaway.

Several software options make putting together an online survey and sharing the link quick and easy—and you can find these tools for free. Research the possibilities and set up your survey to gather some (or all) of the following data with the goal of uncovering the biggest commonalities among your customers:

Gender. Include options for transgender and non-binary customers.

Age. You can give the option to choose age ranges, just don't make them too broad. "Age 25 to 45" doesn't give you as much information as "Age 25 to 30."

Marital or Relationship Status, Kids, Kids' Ages. Finding out who else is in your customer's household can help you understand their priorities. A dad with young kids at home is leading a very different life than a dad with kids in high school.

Opinions about Your Product, Service, or Industry. Be brave and provide an open space for them to answer "What do you like about X?" "What do you dislike about X?," for both your particular offerings and your industry in general.

Traits. If it's useful for your understanding of your audience, ask them to choose traits they consider applicable to themselves:

> "Extrovert; introvert; a little of both."

> "I'm the first to try new things; I like to wait and see if new things really work before trying them."

> "I regularly treat myself; I don't treat myself as often as I'd like."

These kinds of survey questions can give you a lot of insight into the lives of your customers. Really take some time thinking them up—and make sure you don't frame any answers as more negative or positive than the others.

Brand Preferences. Ask where they shop, where they eat, what books they read, what TV shows they watch—all of this can be valuable for getting a well-rounded picture of your audience members.

Values. You could even ask people to rank their values in order of importance. Family, friends, and love will always come first for people, but what comes after will really give you insight. Asking them to rank things like growth and self-improvement, career, hobbies, religion, financial comfort, travel, or self-expression will give you insight into what your audience truly cares about.

Anything Else That Pertains to You! Bear in mind that people won't usually want to answer questions that are too personal or too invasive. But certainly add any questions you know will give you special insight.

One important consideration: People are less likely to complete longer surveys, so regardless of length, put your most important questions first.

Case in Point

A grocery store might seem like the prime candidate for an "Our audience is everyone!" brand, but paying attention to shoppers can yield valuable insights.

Through a combination of observing shoppers throughout the day, along with incentivizing shoppers to take quick surveys in exchange for coupons, one particular grocery store discovered these trends:

- As a whole, 65 percent of their shoppers are women. But between the hours of 7 a.m. and 10 a.m. on weekdays, 85 percent of shoppers are women ages 35 to 47, most of whom just dropped off kids at the school around the corner.

- Between 10 a.m. and 1 p.m., the data changes considerably. During that time, 70 percent of shoppers are between the ages of 65 and 80, as retirees come out to do their shopping. Shoppers are evenly split between men and women.

- After 5 p.m., the after-work crowd changes the demographics again, making the average shopper between 35 to 50 years old and changing the women-to-men ratio to 50/50.

The store could also dig into the kinds of purchases customers make, how often they visit the store, whether they're rewards card members—all kinds of data.

Best of all, this information yields amazing opportunities to gear messages to just the right shoppers at just the right times. For example, promotions about kid lunch staples (sandwiches, veggie snack packs, etc.) would be perfect for those 7 a.m. to 10 a.m. shoppers.

KEEP IN MIND

Knowing your audience—understanding who they are, how they live their lives, and what they want—is crucial to crafting messages that will resonate with them. Before you can even think about writing copy, you need to know who you're writing to. And this is how to find out:

Key Takeaways

Your target audience is never "everyone." There's always a smaller subset of people most likely to be interested in you and buy what you sell. You need to find out who those people are.

The more you know about your audience, the better you can write to them. Learn as much about them as you can, from the way they live their lives to their values to their personal likes and dislikes.

If you're not sure—ask. If you can't get this information just by observing your customers, create a survey for them to take.

Action Items

Determine what you need to know. There are a lot of questions you could ask your target audience—figure out what data points are truly relevant to you.

Pull together any data you already have. You may already have more information than you realize about your email subscribers and followers. What comments have they left on your posts, what replies have they sent to your emails? People volunteer more information than you might realize.

Survey your purchasers, subscribers, or followers to learn more. Email questions to your subscribers or post a survey on social media. If you don't have many followers or subscribers, find groups you believe should be your target audience and ask them to take your survey!

CHAPTER 5

PUT YOURSELF IN THE READER'S SHOES

Now that you have an understanding of who makes up your target audience, the time has come to really get into their heads. The more—and deeper—you understand how your audience thinks, feels, and acts, the easier connecting with them through your copy will be.

You may be able to extrapolate a lot about your audience based on what you know about them. For example, if your audience is made up of college students, a reasonable guess would be that they don't have much expendable income but what income they do have will be spent on themselves. And that's certainly useful.

This chapter explores how to learn even a bit more about why your customers do what they do—what motivates them and what matters to them. You're going to start viewing the world (and your messaging!) from standing in your target audience's shoes.

Remember that your copy is not about you. Your copy needs to be about your target audience and what matters to them. Let's get a very good handle on exactly what those things are.

Strategy Session

Wondering exactly how to get in the head of your target audience? Here are a few tips to get you started.

TO-DO LIST

Spend some time just imagining. Grab a notepad so you can jot down ideas and based on what you've learned about your target audience, imagine their lives. What are their challenges, frustrations, hopes, and dreams? Why do they make the choices they do? What do they want? And *why* do they want what they want?

You may find this much easier if your target audience is similar to yourself. For example, if you are a woman who is an executive, you may have an easier time understanding the motivations, needs, and frustrations of young women in their first post-collegiate jobs. If this is not your demographic, though, you can still glean insight by using your imagination and really looking at the world as much as possible from your audience's perspective.

Talk to people in your target audience: in person, over the phone, over a video call. You can imagine all you want, but there's nothing that can validate your ideas—or give you a course correction—like real live conversations with your audience. The vast majority of questions on your call should start with "why," as in "Why does this matter to you?" and "Why did you decide to do that?"

Be gentle and empathetic when you ask your "why" questions because the more you ask, the more you get into personal and emotional territory. Ask with empathy and respect, and you'll learn a lot more from people than you'd expect.

AVOID THESE PITFALLS

Don't make assumptions, especially assumptions based on your perspective. Hearing yourself think, "I would never do that" or "I would definitely do that" regarding a question is a red flag that you're approaching the issue with the wrong attitude. *You* are not necessarily your target audience. Don't start off making assumptions or, worse, judgments about your audience's choices because doing so will bias your research and give you misleading data.

Don't rush. This is an important process and should take some time! Be sure to take plenty of notes as you go, especially when you talk to people directly.

Don't be shy. Schedule the calls! For every copywriter who's afraid of "bothering" people, there are dozens of people in a target audience who'd be honored to be asked for their insight and opinions.

Don't be afraid to dig deeper. Here's a pro tip: After you get the first answer, ask "why" again. And maybe another time after that. Those follow-up "whys" are where the gold is.

For example, a man may tell you that he bought a small motorboat because he wanted to take his grandkids fishing on the weekends. Okay, great: Why is that important? Well, because he remembers fishing with his grandfather. And why is that important? Because he wants his grandkids to have the same wonderful memories of him after he's gone. Boom: There's the gold. He's not buying a boat just to fish; he's buying a boat to create a bond with his grandchildren and secure happy memories after he's passed away.

Case in Point

An online houseplant sales and delivery company wants to understand the perspective of its target audience. Their largest demographic is people ages 28 to 35 who live alone or with one roommate or a partner. The gender breakdown is almost 50/50, and 75 percent of their customers live in or near urban centers in apartments or condos under 900 square feet.

Their marketing director schedules phone calls with their top customers to help understand what drives purchases. Here's roughly how the average conversation went:

Marketing Director: Have your plant purchases been for you or someone else?

Customer: Mostly for me.

MD: And why have you decided to make those purchases?

C: Oh, I just like how they look.

MD: That's interesting. And why does that matter to you?

C: Well, I guess it's just kind of nice to have real greenery in the house.

MD: Absolutely. And why does *that* matter to you?

C: Hmm . . . I guess having plants around is just soothing. With them, I can turn my apartment into an oasis. The city is so loud and busy; it's nice to come home and see the plants.

As the marketing director discovered, the real motivation for purchasing plants wasn't just that customers wanted their apartments to look pretty. They were trying to create a calm and soothing personal sanctuary for themselves to combat the chaos of city life.

This perspective will allow the company's copywriter to craft vastly more insightful, resonating, and effective copy to reach and connect with their target audience and drive new or additional purchases.

Key Takeaways

Get out of your own head. Be very careful about judging your target audience or ascribing their behavior based on your own perspective.

If you're not 100 percent positive, ask. You can make educated, empathetic guesses, but don't make assumptions. The best way to get your target audience's perspective is to ask.

Keep asking. People (and groups) evolve. Talking to your target audience once is not enough. Check in at least once a year, or more frequently, especially when big events or circumstances may be affecting them.

Action Items

Do some brainstorming from your audience's perspective. Spend time with the information you've gathered about your audience and really try to imagine what being in their circumstances would be like. Take notes about what you envision them thinking and feeling. You may not always be spot on, but going through this process is a great way to start developing a connection with your audience.

Schedule calls with people who buy your product or use your service. If you have an email list, send out a request to set up quick calls to learn more about their wants and needs. If you don't, ask family, friends, and colleagues if they know anyone who falls in your target audience. Chances are they'll know at least a few.

Dig deeper to get at the emotion. When you interview people, ask a lot of "why" questions and don't stop at just one. Gently and respectfully asking some form of "And why is that?" to a series of questions can help unearth deeper motivations and values your audience themselves might not even have been aware of.

CHAPTER 6

UNDERSTAND YOUR PRODUCT'S BENEFITS AND FEATURES

At the risk of sounding hyperbolic, there's nothing you can do for your copywriting that will have more impact than identifying the benefit of your offer and conveying that offer well to your audience. Nothing.

Why? Well, no one takes action—signs up for something, makes a purchase, changes their mind—if doing so doesn't benefit them in some way. When you can convey what that way is, as clearly as possible, the chance that somebody will take the action you want them to take increases exponentially.

Now, there is one small caveat: Separating an offering's *benefits* from its *features* can sometimes be tricky. Many an ad or piece of copy has tried to highlight the benefits of an item and failed miserably because it mistakenly focused on features instead.

So, in this section, we're going to get crystal clear on the difference between features and benefits. Once you learn that, you can be sure you're always focusing on what *truly* matters to your audience.

Strategy Session

People don't buy products, they buy transformations. This phrase is repeated so often, we no longer know who first crafted these words. That it resonates with so many people is a testament to its truth.

No one wants to buy a tractor, or a new phone, or a face cream, or a health coaching package—what they *want* is the positive change in their life that will come from that purchase. And that's why focusing on benefits is so crucial to writing effective copy.

A **benefit** is what makes a product useful to someone—the value the product has for them. A benefit answers the consumer's question "What's in it for me?" and promises change. (Note that "product" in this context might mean a tangible item that you sell, or a service you provide, or even a membership to the nonprofit you're writing for. In broader terms, you'll also begin thinking about the benefits of taking actions you want people to take, but let's keep things simple for a bit.)

A **feature** is a detail about the product. Here's an example: The *feature* of a new razor could be "This razor now has seven blades!" But the *benefit* is "Get the closest and smoothest shave that no other razor can provide." In the end, the consumer is not all that concerned that the razor has seven blades or nine or three; what really matters is that they can get the closest and smoothest shave they've ever had.

Getting caught up in features, especially ones that fall into the "new," "better," and "special" categories, can be very easy to do. But to a prospective purchaser, terms like "new," "better," and "special" don't mean anything unless they're tied to something the customer values.

Features can be very useful to support or expand on the main message of the benefit, but they're not a substitute for the benefit itself.

Benefits serve the dual purpose of reminding customers of problems they already have and demonstrating how the particular product or service can solve those problems. Good copywriting, then, is powerful because it creates the perfect match. You tell people exactly how your product can solve their problem and that gets people to purchase from you. This way, you address their needs without them even having to ask.

You need to figure out the benefit for any copy project. If you want someone to sign up for an email list, what's the benefit for them? If you want someone to open an email, what are they going to get out of doing so? If you want someone to contact you to set up a free evaluation, what's the value to them?

Discerning between benefits and features can take a little practice but here's how to start honing that skill. Ask yourself:

1   What's the general purpose of the product?

2   How do any new enhancements make what I'm offering better?

3   What problem does the product solve?

4   How does this solution help the consumer?

5   And then how does your answer to #4 help them? And how does your answer to this question help them? And so on.

What you're trying to get at is the deepest need of the consumer and the most essential way that your product helps them. For example, consider a new brand of mascara:

1   What's the general purpose? To add length to someone's eyelashes.

2   How do new enhancements make their application better? A new applicator design is easier and quicker to use.

3   What problem does the design solve? Someone who's in a rush or running late won't have to spend as much time applying mascara.

4   How does this convenience help consumers? They save time and still look good.

5 And how does saving time and still looking good help them? They can feel more attractive and confident in less time *and* feel less stressed when they're getting ready.

Case in Point

To make sure you've got a good grasp on benefits versus features, try this quick quiz. For each line below, determine whether the copy describes a benefit or a feature and why. Then check the answers that follow to see how you did.

- Protect your family from intruders at all times.
- Easily compare prices across multiple sites!
- Never have a bad hair day.
- Get real-time details about stock trades and quotes.
- Same products. Lower prices.
- Softens clothes while they dry!

Protect your family from intruders at all times.

BENEFIT!

Protecting oneself and one's family is one of the most basic human desires and promising that outcome is one of the most powerful benefits to offer a consumer.

Easily compare prices across multiple sites!

FEATURE!

Statements that have verbs in the first one or two words can *sound* like a benefit and with the concept of "prices" in there, getting tripped up is easy. But when you think about the wording a bit, you realize that "comparing prices" isn't the end benefit; the end benefit is finding the lowest price. With a feature statement like this, often just asking yourself why will yield the true benefit.

Never have a bad hair day.

BENEFIT!

This is a little tricky because the message is worded negatively, but try rephrasing the sentence in the positive: Always have great hair. This benefit may not be especially deep or noble but it certainly speaks to everyone's desire to be attractive.

Get real-time details about stock trades and quotes.

FEATURE!

"Real-time details" sure sounds impressive but these details are not an end result. Often feature statements lead you to ask, "So, what would *that* get me?" A possible benefit might be "Make better trade decisions and increase the value of your investment accounts."

Same products. Lower prices.

BENEFIT!

This statement is simple but no less beneficial. The promise is you get the same products for less, meaning you'll save money, which is a very big and very powerful benefit.

Softens clothes while they dry!

FEATURE!

Just because you can infer a benefit right away (Save time! Save effort! Comfy clothes!) doesn't mean the statement isn't a feature. You had to make that connection in your head instead of seeing the words in the copy, and some potential buyers might not make this connection at all. Rephrasing this statement slightly, this copy basically says that a clothes dryer has an added feature that also softens clothes.

Not only is understanding and highlighting the benefit of your project the most substantial thing you can do to increase the effectiveness of your copy, failure to do so almost always accounts for a copy project going wrong.

Think of the concept this way: If you don't make clear to people what they're going to get out of a product or service, they'll never take the time and energy to figure out the benefit themselves. They don't need to bother because there are so many other competitors for their attention (and their money!). When you don't make the benefit crystal clear, you miss out on an opportunity. And for a potentially large segment of your audience, you may not get another chance.

Key Takeaways

Benefits are your copy's magic bullets. Well, okay, maybe not "magic bullets" exactly, but as close to magic as you can get. When you convey the benefit for your readers, they become invested, and they're much more likely to take the action you want them to take.

Features support your benefits. Features are important, too. They can help support the claim that your benefit makes. Often features give further insight into how the benefit helps your target audience.

Lead with benefits, follow up with features. If you think of your features as supporting your benefit, you'll never go wrong with your messaging hierarchy. There certainly are more advanced copywriters who have the skills to change this order, but at this stage in your learning, stick with the tried and true. Walk before you run.

Action Items

Identify the ONE main benefit for the project you're writing. Remember, you want to keep your message clear and focused so make sure you're writing about a single, significant benefit.

Experiment with a few different ways of writing about the benefit. There are always going to be at least a few ways to convey an idea. Before you settle on one, try playing around with how you present your benefit to your audience. Often you may need a few iterations to get the copy just right.

List three features that support the claim your benefit makes. Eventually you'll incorporate your features into your subheads and body copy; more on that to come (see page 64). For now, just list three features that best support the benefit you've highlighted.

The Creative Brief

There's one key element of the copywriting process we haven't addressed yet: the creative brief.

The creative brief is a single document that contains all the key information, goals, and parameters about a project—everything we've been discussing. The brief helps the copywriter stay focused on what they need to create. When working with a client, the document helps ensure that the copywriter and client see eye to eye from the very beginning.

Every copywriting project should begin with a creative brief. Every. Single. One. When a project falls apart, 99 percent of the time there wasn't a creative brief or the brief wasn't thoughtfully filled out.

So why have I waited so long to introduce this concept? Because you just learned how to identify almost all the elements that will go into the brief, and that's what's most important.

Following are a few of the key questions your creative brief *must* address, but don't let this requirement limit you. As you dig into the project and answer these questions, if they prompt more questions, great! The more thinking you do before you begin writing, the better your project will be.

CREATIVE BRIEF

What kind of project is this? Email, website, direct mail, etc.

To whom are we communicating? Who's the target audience?

What is the one main thing we want them to do? What's the action we want them to take after reading the copy?

What's the benefit for them? What do they get out of doing the action? What's in it for them?

What features support that benefit? What are the details about the product?

What are the business objectives this project was designed to meet? How will they be measured? More subscribers, more purchasers, more page viewers, etc.

What is the brand tone? More on this in chapter 16 (see pages 102 to 106).

And here's a bonus piece of advice my team and I give to our students: Never skip the brief!

CHAPTER 7

HONE YOUR HOOK

There's a reason why fishermen use hooks instead of just, oh, say, tying an expertly constructed knot around the worm. Because the worm—the bait, the main meal—is only half of what gets that fish out of the water and into the boat.

The other half is the hook. Apologies to the squeamish or those with particular affinities for fish, but the hook is what actually *catches* the fish and allows the angler to reel it in.

The hook in your copywriting performs the same function. An effective hook, as the first line or two of a piece of copy, catches the reader's attention and entices them to read more. The hook grabs them and helps you reel them in.

The sad truth is that people won't read all of the copy you put out into the world, so catching your audience's attention with a great hook is crucial. This hook is what engages them, interests them, and increases the chances they'll read the rest of your amazing message.

Let's explore how to create effective hooks of your own!

Strategy Session

Hooks come into play in longer pieces of copy and content: body copy, social media captions, blog posts. Before we start brainstorming different hooks and different directions, though, there's one point I want to make clear:

> Your hook has to relate to the main message of that piece of copy.

If you start off with a fascinating story about how your grandmother lost her teeth in a riverboat accident, then start talking about the massage therapy treatments at your spa . . . your reader will be lost. And, worse, they'll stop reading.

But if you follow that story with information about your emergency dental services or the importance of seat belts on mobile water-faring casinos, your reader will make the connection and keep reading.

Another quick note before we get into the discussion:

> Your hook must be genuinely interesting.

When in doubt, ask yourself if you'd keep reading. Or even better, ask an honest friend (ideally, also one in your target audience) if they'd keep reading. If the answer is "meh," go back to the drawing board.

HOW TO CRAFT AN IRRESISTIBLE HOOK

Take a narrative approach. People naturally love stories and crave following them to their conclusion. So start compiling a roster of narratives you can draw on when writing your copy. Begin by making a list of interesting or unusual stories and experiences from your life.

Then, add interesting or unusual stories from the lives of your friends or family members. As long as those friends or family members don't mind, those stories are free to use. (Change names, dates, and other details to protect your loved ones' privacy.)

You can even expand your story library to include anecdotes you've heard about others. Just make sure you're not infringing on anyone's privacy or intellectual property and be certain you get the story right.

Round out your list with any metaphors you regularly use to explain elements of your business—or any metaphors that can help people understand a key concept in your messaging. For example, I often use the TV show *The Bachelor* as a metaphor for why freelancers don't tend to thrive when they use job bidding sites to find work: Being the Bachelor himself is great, but your odds of success are low when you're competing as one of the 25 women.

Build suspense. People love stories because of the beginning, middle, and . . .

Aren't you just dying for me to finish that statement? Of course you are: That's how humans are wired. When someone opens up an information loop, we naturally crave closure. So use the beginning and middle of a compelling story as your hook and save the end until the very end of your copy, and you'll get people to keep reading. They've just got to know how the story turns out!

Go for shock value. Anything that makes people think to themselves "Whoa—what??" has the potential to be a great hook. Surprising and pertinent facts about your topic can do double duty, hooking people as well as opening their eyes to a problem, concept, or idea they were previously unaware of.

Similarly, if you have an opinion or piece of advice that's directly opposed to what most people are saying, this tidbit can make a great hook. Don't be controversial just for controversy's sake, but an unusual opinion or piece of advice can both attract attention and help build faith in your expertise.

Point out what's unique. No matter what business you're in, competitors are trying to take your customers. So why should people choose you? Always have the answer to this question at the ready. And how you answer that question can also make for some great hooks. What is unique about you? What's unique about your business? What do you bring to the table that no one else does?

Case in Point

A local independent movie theater wants to publicize its new "Fright Night" events with a series of social media posts. Every Friday night, the movie theater is showing a classic horror film at midnight, and it is looking for an interesting way to get people excited AND to buy tickets.

Here's their original strategy for social media posts:

Get tickets for Fright Night! Every Friday at midnight we'll show one of our favorite horror films. Link in bio to buy your tickets. Don't miss out!

And whereas this approach was, well, *okay* . . . the copy wasn't great. (Notice how it missed the benefit completely?) Taking a second (ahem) stab at it, the theater decided to play with a hook. Here's what it went with:

Not every odd kid turns out to be a homicidal maniac. Not every summer camp is stalked by a lunatic. And not every dream turns into a nightmare . . . that kills. But, great news: Every Friday this month, they will!

Freak yourself out every Friday at midnight and see four classic horror movies the way they were meant to be seen: On the big screen! Get your tickets now. It's frightening just how fast they'll sell out!

Maximum 2 tickets per person, buy now at the link in our bio!

The second piece of copy leads with an attention-grabbing hook that also inspires the right target audience (horror-film buffs) to take action.

The rest of your copy is virtually irrelevant if your hook doesn't draw the audience in. You have their attention for just a few moments; use a powerful hook to keep them reading to the end of your message.

Key Takeaways

A hook catches your target audience's attention and pulls them in. At the beginning of a longer piece of copy or content, a great hook attracts interest and stops your reader from moving on to the next thing.

Hooks must be genuinely interesting. The first line doesn't count as a hook if people don't actually get hooked. Be objective with your writing and evaluate whether your hook truly is remarkable, disruptive, or thought-provoking.

Hooks must relate to the rest of the message. There's no point in catching someone's attention with a hook that doesn't pertain strongly to the message you're conveying. If you catch them with the hook, you'll lose them when your copy pivots to a totally unrelated topic.

Action Items

Figure out the main message you're trying to convey. Figuring out this message is the first step when writing a hook.

Review the strategy session in this chapter to brainstorm possible hooks. Knowing your main message, what interesting stories or metaphors, shocking or surprising facts, opinions, advice, or points of uniqueness could you use to create a hook?

Narrow down your options by choosing the hook that is both the most interesting and the most directly related to your main message.

CHAPTER 8

KEEP READERS' ATTENTION

After you've caught your reader's attention with a great hook, the process is all easy from there, right? Oh, if only that were the case! Catching their attention is only half the battle; the other half is keeping their focus. Once your target audience starts reading, plenty of distractions can lure them away if they don't stay invested in your message.

This chapter suggests several tactics to ensure your target audience reads as much copy as possible and, even more importantly, they absorb your key pieces of information and take the action you want them to take.

Strategy Session

I'll be honest: Catching people's attention is generally much easier than keeping their focus. After all, most people are willing to give up a moment of their time to read something interesting. But keeping their attention for multiple moments—or even minutes—is something entirely different.

Fundamentally, keeping people's attention comes down to giving them pertinent, valuable information without your message getting bogged down by anything extraneous. The only messaging in your copy should be that which gives the reader more reason to take the action you want them to take.

Sounds simple, right? And the concept is—but the practice is not. What is easy is the opposite: packing in all kinds of other messaging "in case the audience needs more information or context," because you haven't really thought through what you truly need to say. Or worst of all, because you just like the sound of those unnecessary sentences you wrote.

Remember, as much as we copywriters wish people would read everything we write, they just won't. Which is why keeping your message clear and free of any extra information is so important: You want whatever they *do* read to matter. Here's how to ensure they get the main message:

DO: Decide what action you want people to take. What's the purpose of this piece? Why does what you're telling them matter? What's the desired end result?

DON'T: Forget where people are in the customer journey. When people read this piece, are they familiar with the brand? Were they led to this message via previous interactions? What do they already know? What choices did they make, what needs did they identify to get to this messaging?

DO: Figure out what key points will get them from the beginning of your copy to the end. What do they *really* need to know to take the action you want them to take? What superfluous information gets in their way?

DON'T: Write just for writing's sake. Any extra messaging is just a distraction and, worse, risks losing your reader. Be ruthless in critiquing your own messaging. What *needs* to be there?

DO: Create a progression with your messages. A leads to B leads to C leads to your Desired End Result. The messages you include should make sense together and should lead readers from one to the next in a natural progression to your call to action. Anything that gets in the way of this flow has to go.

DON'T: Skip writing an outline. This step is one most copy-writers overlook—and that's a giant mistake. Whenyour key points of messaging are laid out on a page you can reference, staying focused on saying what you need to say is much easier. Keeping those points only in your head is an invitation to go off on tangents and let other, less important points creep in.

DO: Plan time for editing. We'll talk more about editing in chapter 12, but, for now, keep in mind that editing is crucial for writing copy that keeps the reader's attention. When writing your first draft, you simply need to get something down on the page. More than likely, the result is pretty far from perfect. Fine! That's what editing is for. When you go back through your draft, you'll look at what you've written with a discerning eye to make sure you really did stick to only the most crucial points. If anything you've written is distracting for the reader, delete!

Case in Point

An online weight-loss coach was trying to create a sales page for her one-on-one coaching business. Her audience would only get to this sales page after going through a multi-email funnel (see chapter 18, page 112) in which she introduced herself, described what makes her coaching different, and shared a few client success stories.

Based on this plan, she knew these things:

- Visitors to the sales page were interested in weight loss.

- They were interested enough in learning about her program to click the link to the page.

- They were at least somewhat familiar with who she was.

But she also knew that not everyone reads every email, so not everyone reading the sales page will have seen all of the messages in her email funnel.

Her intent for this page: to get people to purchase her one-on-one coaching program.

Where the readers are in the customer journey: interested in weight loss and familiar with her but not yet committed to making a purchase.

The key points her audience needs to know:

- The benefit (Her coaching helps people lose weight much more effectively than other methods.)

- Other clients' results (client success stories)

- What kinds of results the reader can expect to see

- Whom the program is a good fit for

- Why she's qualified to offer this program (her origin story)

- What's included in the coaching package

- Her guarantee

- How long they have to buy before the offer expires

- The price

What's she's *not* going to include:

- The benefits of weight loss (The readers already want weight loss so she doesn't have to sell them on this point!)

- Anything about her self-paced weight-loss course, which is a totally different product.

- Details about her corporate career and MBA

- Details about other diets people may or may not have already tried (These stories would distract from her main message.)

On the basis of this message planning, she creates an outline for a highly focused and engaging sales page.

In school, a lot of writing was about packing your essays to get to a certain word count. Copywriting is the exact opposite—you want to strip away messaging that's not essential to make your point, convey your brand, and get the reader to do what you want to them to do.

Key Takeaways

Keeping your reader engaged is difficult. I won't sugarcoat this point; cracking this skill is going to be the hardest part for many copywriters. But doing so is much easier when you stay focused on what really needs to be said.

Don't let your own copy distract the reader. Once you've gotten a reader's attention, the biggest danger of losing their focus is in your own copy. If messaging moves into areas that a reader doesn't need to know, already knows, or is off-topic, that reader is very likely to leave.

Include only what's essential to get them to take action. Be ruthless in editing your messaging. Sure, there's plenty that you *could* include in a piece but very little that you actually *need* to.

Action Items

List your essential key points. The best defense against throwing in extra messaging is being clear on what you want to say from the outset. Make a list of your key points before you start writing, and check what you've written frequently.

Make sure each point leads to the next. An effective piece of copy isn't just a jumble of statements; each point should lead naturally to the next, so that taking the desired action at the end is practically inevitable.

Strip out anything that gets in the way. Being objective with your own copy is hard, but this objectivity is also part of the job. After you've created your first draft, go through and remove anything that distracts from your key points.

CHAPTER 9

STRUCTURE YOUR COPY FOR READABILITY

I n the last chapter, you whittled down your copy into only the most essential elements. Great work—that's a huge milestone! But now the time has arrived to make sure the structure of your copy supports the effort to get people to read as much as possible.

No matter how interested someone is in a topic, they're going to be averse to reading long paragraphs and long sentences. Long paragraphs look daunting and dense. Long sentences challenge readers to remember your first point by the time they get to the end.

And with copywriting, especially, people don't want to (and won't!) put in much effort to understand your point. So this chapter will teach you to structure your copy, making what you write as inviting and easy to consume as possible.

Strategy Session

Thanks to the previous chapters, you have a lot of tools at your disposal to help make your copy much more inviting to the reader. Those same tools will also help with conveying your message. This session goes over how to get through to your readers with as many key points as possible, even if they choose not to read every word. When it comes to reading, some people are skimmers. This section teaches you how to make your copy more readable *and* how to communicate to people who only skim.

Let's talk about the key elements you have to work with.

Headlines. The headline is generally the first and most important copy the reader will see. Like a headline in a newspaper, the headlines in your copy are usually at the top, and the type is usually a larger size than the rest of the copy. The headline tells the story of what's on the rest of the page so if someone didn't read anything but the headline, they'd still have a good idea of what the whole page is about. You'll almost always want to put your benefit in the headline. And—this is key—there's only *one* headline on a page. So make those words work hard.

Subheads. Subheads (or subheadlines) are just what they sound like: smaller, less important headlines. A subhead right after a headline supplies any additional supporting information needed to make the headline impactful. If you have a lot of messages to convey, use subheads to highlight each one them. Your subheads convey the overarching message of each section. When skimming your copy, a reader should be able to get the gist of what you're trying to say solely by reading the headline and subheads.

Short paragraphs. Remember, this is not English class and you're not writing a composition. Instead of packing as much into each paragraph as you can, you should be looking to break up your paragraphs. None should be more than two or three lines long!

Short sentences. Short sentences make readers happy. And they increase retention! Here's what happens when you try to pack too much into a long sentence: Readers have to remember everything from the beginning all the way to the end. More often than not, they don't retain any part. Are your sentences long? You're trying to pack too many concepts into them. Break them up!

Bullet points. Bullet points (or just bullets) are lists of information, so-called because of the typography element (•) often used to denote them. Bullets can make information easy to consume, but don't overuse them. They should only appear when you have a list of three or more points, all of which fall into the same category. Use bulleted lists sparingly; they're a tool and are not the only choice.

Call-out boxes. I won't get too much into design here (that's what designers are for). But depending on the piece, you may sometimes want to call out particular copy in some special way. Maybe you put a literal box in a top corner (called a "Johnson Box" in the direct-mail world), or maybe you place copy in a sidebar on a website; the idea is to separate out important, but not directly related, copy, like statistics or quotes from happy customers.

Case in Point

A house cleaner was looking to improve the effectiveness of a flyer he created to advertise his special deep-cleaning service. He leaves flyers in mailboxes and gives some to his clients to share with their friends. His original copy was:

DEEP CLEANING FOR HOUSES

Get that squeaky-clean feeling from floor to ceiling—without lifting a finger! Book a deep-cleaning appointment to make your home shine. Too tired or overwhelmed to clean? Let me help! A one-time deep-cleaning appointment gets into the nooks and crannies everyday cleaning doesn't. Your appointment includes everything in a standard cleaning, plus oven cleaning, refrigerator cleaning, mattress rotating, floor cleaning and polishing, wall-washing, inside and outside window-cleaning, and linens laundering even if you don't have a washer and dryer. Special services available on request. Cross it off your to-do list and give yourself the gift of a perfectly clean house! Call Houston Whole-House Cleaners at 555-5555 to schedule your appointment today.

From Kim H, one of our happy clients: "I have never seen my house this clean! And the HWH team was so fast, courteous, and thorough. I can't recommend them highly enough. I don't know why I waited so long!" Additional references available upon request.

Here's how he reformatted the text:

GET THAT SQUEAKY-CLEAN FEELING FROM FLOOR TO CEILING—WITHOUT LIFTING A FINGER!
Book a deep-cleaning appointment to make your home shine.

Too tired or overwhelmed to clean? Let us help!

A one-time deep-cleaning appointment gets into the nooks and crannies everyday cleaning doesn't. Your appointment includes everything in a standard cleaning, plus:

- Oven cleaning
- Refrigerator cleaning
- Mattress rotating
- Floor cleaning and polishing
- Wall-washing
- Inside and outside window-cleaning
- Linens laundering (even if you don't have a washer and dryer!)
- Special services available on request

Cross it off your to-do list and give yourself the gift of a perfectly clean house!

Call Houston Whole-House Cleaners at 555-5555 to schedule your appointment today.

"I have never seen my house this clean! And the HWH team was so fast, courteous, and thorough. I can't recommend them highly enough. I don't know why I waited so long!"
—Kim H, a happy Houston Whole-House Cleaners Client.

As you can see, his new layout made the whole process much easier for readers. In this format, they can digest the information, find the messages pertinent to them, and, of course, take action and book appointments.

KEEP IN MIND

With copy that looks easy to read, the chances that people will actually read what you've written increases! Use these tips to structure your copy and organize your messaging.

Key Takeaways

Headlines and subheads anchor your messages. These are the main building blocks of your copy, so use them wisely.

Keep paragraphs and sentences short. No one wants to read long paragraphs. Or long sentences. So don't make them! Keep things short.

Use bullets and other formatting, but do so sparingly. These tools can be great but are distracting if overused. Focus first on keeping your copy concise, and then use these formatting options where you need to.

Action Items

Evaluate your headline and subhead(s). Are they doing the heavy lifting to convey your message? If not, time to revise.

Break up your paragraphs and sentences. You shouldn't have any more than two or three lines per paragraph. Your sentences should only contain one idea apiece.

Evaluate opportunities for bullets and other formatting. Your copy may not need these tools but know that you've got them in your back pocket.

CHAPTER 10

MASTER YOUR CALL TO ACTION

Right after graduating from college, I worked at a health club. The sales trainer there once asked me if I knew the number-one reason most people didn't join a gym after taking a tour. I guessed the price. Wrong. Maybe they're afraid they wouldn't use the membership or that the distance from the gym to their homes was too long? Both were wrong.

He told me the number-one reason people don't join after they get a tour is that the salesperson *never actually asks them if they want to join.* People don't take action if we don't tell them which action to take, whether when touring health clubs or when reading copy.

This chapter focues on crafting clear directions for your reader—what we call the call to action (CTA). Instead of letting your reader languish in confusion, you'll tell them exactly what to do next. The tactics laid out here will vastly increase the chance for success in this regard.

Strategy Session

In many ways, the copywriter acts as a compass for the reader. You as the copywriter are a guide for every person who reads your copy. Through the whole interaction, your copy must show the reader where to go and give them clues about where they're headed.

This strategy session won't be a long one because this shouldn't be complicated. Ask yourself:

What is the next step? What is the action you want your reader to take? What is the desired outcome of this copy piece?

How can you convey your message in the simplest way?

Is what happens next clear from this copy?

CRAFTING YOUR CTA

DON'T get cute with your calls to action. You need to ensure that your reader is completely clear about the meaning of your call to action. Skip "Add this dynamo to your shopping cart!" in favor of "Buy Now" or "Add to Shopping Cart." Your reader is going to be scanning the page for familiar copy in the CTA. When they want to buy, they'll look for "Buy Now."

DON'T make your reader do unnecessary thinking. "Click here to read more" is easy to understand. "Let's get this show going!" isn't. What show? Going where? Wait, is the rest of the article here or do I need to keep reading somewhere else? Too much thinking involved.

DO make what's going to happen next very clear. When people click "Buy Now" they expect to be taken to a cart page. But what about "Let's Chat"? Will they be taken to a scheduling app, will they be taken to a "Contact Us" page, or will they be taken to a chat box with customer service?

Let people know where they're going and what to expect. "Schedule Your Appointment Now!" should take them to an opportunity to schedule an appointment. "Find Out More" should take them to a place with more details. The more confused people are, the less likely they'll take the action you want from them.

DO keep your hierarchy clear if multiple CTAs are required. A person can only take one next step so there should be only one CTA. But you've likely seen emails or webpages that seem to break that rule. An evite invites you to RSVP but also to "See the Guest List" or "Add to Calendar." The key is that RSVPing is *the most prominent CTA* and is the most recommended next step.

(For increased clarity and impact, could you make the RSVP the one call to action, saving "See the Guest List" and "Add to Calendar" for other pages and places in the customer journey? Very likely.)

Case in Point

Sometimes your CTA will be in a button and sometimes in a line of copy. (And sometimes both, which is fine—as long as the action is the same!) As a broad rule, a line that begins with a verb is a call to action.

Let's explore a few common CTAs and see what works and what doesn't.

"Schedule Your Massage Service Now"
This makes sense if your user is taken to a scheduling page but doesn't make sense if your user is taken to a contact form. ("Contact Us to Schedule Your Massage" would be a good choice in that scenario.)

"Add to Cart"
This works if an item is added to the shopping cart and the user stays on the same page. If the user is taken to the cart page, this button won't work because the user won't be expecting to go there!

"Discover Laser Light Therapy"

This one isn't terrible but takes some extrapolation. The user can reasonably assume they'll get more details after the click . . . but why make people think? Keep the process simple. "Learn More about Laser Light Therapy" is so much clearer.

"Give Me the Sales Training Video for Just $7!"

This interesting variation is one you'll see (or use) most often on buttons. The copy is still a call to action but acts as if the reader is calling themselves to action. The alternative would be "Get the Sales Training Video for Just $7!" Both are clear, and the user could reasonably expect to be taken to a cart page. Whether a first-person "Give Me" or a second-person "Get" will be right for you depends on the brand as well as on testing. (More on testing coming up, see page 95.)

KEEP IN MIND

Don't overcomplicate your call to action! Keep your message simple and straightforward—just let people know what their next step is.

Key Takeaways

People don't take action if you don't tell them to. Don't make people guess or hunt—they won't. Just tell them their next step.

Keep your CTA simple. Keep your language straightforward and clear; your CTA is not the place to get cutesy or complicated.

Make sure people know what's going to happen next. Your CTA needs to directly connect to the next place the user is going or to what's happening next.

Action Items

Choose the one next step you want people to take. Remember, one person can't go down two paths at once! What do you want them to do?

Write out your message. Don't get fancy—just put your copy on the page.

Test your message for clarity. You think what you write is clear, but will other people? Poll a few friends or coworkers to find out what they think the CTA means and what they think will happen after they take action. Got your message right? Great. Got it wrong? Time to revise.

CHAPTER 11

CREATE YOUR COPY DOC

Every type of writing adheres to a kind of formatting that helps guide how the work comes to life. Screenwriting and playwriting, for example, each follow specific guidelines that help the director and actors know what was intended with each line and each direction.

Copywriting is no different. You need to format your copywriting document—your copy doc—so that a designer can know what each line and section represent. After all, how can they know which line in your copy doc is the headline if you don't tell them? You don't want them to have to guess.

Even if you're designing your own work (not necessarily recommended but sometimes necessary) or you're writing a text-only email, you still need to clearly delineate what is what. This chapter delves into how to create a neat and tidy copy doc and makes all of your copy choices crystal clear.

A note: Once you get comfortable with copy formatting, you may choose to start formatting at the outline stage rather than inserting the formatting after you're done writing. Find what works best for you.

Strategy Session

I have two overarching pieces of advice as you prepare your copy doc:

Don't overcomplicate. The format of your copy doc should be simple and easy for anyone to understand.

Don't try to design. Your copy doc is not the place to demonstrate font sizes or colors or make recommendations about images or layouts. When you share your copy doc with your designer, they'll do what they do best and put your copy into design. Then, you two can collaborate to make changes. Even if you're designing for yourself (again, not necessarily recommended), you shouldn't be including design thoughts or elements at this stage. Get your copy nailed down first, then square away your design.

There are a few different ways to format your copy doc, but I'll share the most common approach I've come across, which is the one I use. Follow the steps below in order to format after you've written your copy, or format as you go (my personal preference because doing so helps me organize my thoughts).

1 **Put the formatting labels right above the copy they refer to.** Pretty simple. If you're labeling a headline, keep that headline label right above your actual headline copy. Same thing for body copy, subheads, etc. Each label applies to all the copy that follows, until you're ready to move on to the next label. This ensures clarity in what each label refers to.

2 **Note your different elements and sections and use all caps to call them out.** You don't need fancy fonts or colors or to change the size of the type, just write out the labels in all caps. HEADLINE is a clear and simple label for your headline copy. "But what if I intend my actual headline copy to be all caps? Won't that be confusing?" Nope . . . because

the word "HEADLINE" before a line will always mean headline copy is following, no matter the format.

3   **Identify the buttons in your doc and use brackets to note them.** If you intend for your copy to have a button somewhere (arguably the only design element you can denote), put the copy for the button in brackets: [Buy Now] or [Sign Me Up!]

4   **Add bold formatting ONLY if you need to denote major sections within a doc.** If you're putting together a large copy doc, say for a website with multiple pages, then bolding to denote a new section is appropriate. Keep it simple, though: Boldface just the name or type of page ("About Us Page") and then get back to the standard non-bolded type.

5   **Give your doc a final look-over to make sure you've used the type styles you intend for the finished product.** If you want all your headlines to have capitalization at the start of each important word (e.g., This Is a Headline), then write up your copy doc that way. Similarly, don't use ampersands if you mean "and" and don't use any shorthand you don't want in the final product. Your designer isn't a copy editor; they'll often copy and paste the text you give them right into their design software.

6   **When you're done with the draft, use the comments feature to add notes or call things out.** If you have additional information you want to share or notes you want to make sure someone sees, use the comments feature of your word processing app. Don't put notes into the doc itself. The doc should *only* contain copy and labels. Including anything else adds confusion. If you want to, say, offer up another subject line for your client to test, or note which page a link should go to, use a comments box.

Case in Point

Here are a few examples of how a copy doc and copy formatting can look for different projects:

FOR AN EMAIL

SUBJECT LINE
Here's $25 to Welcome You Back!

SNIPPET/PRE-HEADER
Tell Us All about Your Trip! Take Our Short Survey and Get a $25 Credit.

HEADLINE
Get $25 to Tell Us about Your Trip

SUBHEAD
Welcome Back! We Have Two Quick Questions for You.

BODY
Would you please fill out our very short survey? It will take about two minutes of your time, bring you tons of good karma—and get you a $25 credit toward your next trip!

[Take the Survey]

FOR A DIRECT MAIL POSTCARD

SIDE 1

HEADLINE
The Easiest Money-Saving Step You'll Take

SUBHEAD
Let Acme Corporation Take Over Your Accounting Tasks

BOX
Small Businesses Benefiting from Acme Right Now:

- Hair salons
- Coffee shops
- Bars and restaurants
- Retail stores

HEADLINE
A Customized Program with Uncommon Savings

BODY
Acme Creates a Unique Accounting Program for You That Includes:

- Full administrative support
- All tax preparation and filing
- Payroll administration
- Audit protection

Call Acme at 555-555-5555 now for your free consultation!

FOR A WEBPAGE BANNER AD

FRAME 1
A London Hotel That's Utterly Posh . . .

FRAME 2
. . . For Half the Price.

FRAME 3
Say Cheeri-o to the Hayden Arms Hotel.

[Book Now!]

Remember that your copy doc doesn't have to be perfect—the greatest goal is just that all parts be clear. If you understand what you mean and, importantly, your designer understands what you mean, your copy doc has been successful.

Formatting your copy doc should be the easiest part of your copywriting project. Don't overthink and complicate!

Key Takeaways

Keep your message simple, straightforward, and consistent. The goal is that someone unfamiliar with the project can pick up your copy doc and immediately understand what's what. The simpler you keep your doc, the more likely all will be clear.

Don't try to design in your copy doc. Your copy doc is for one thing: Your copy. The copy doc is the blueprint, not the artistic rendering. Wait until you're collaborating with your designer (or taking that design step yourself) to start thinking about layout and type treatments. Get your messaging nailed down first.

Use comments to add notes. Keep your copy doc text strictly for copy; use comments for any suggestions, questions, options, etc.

Action Items

Identify the different sections in your copy doc. Before you can label your copy, you need to be clear on what you intended for each line of copy.

Label them clearly. Don't get fancy and don't complicate things. Use clear, all caps labels: HEADLINE, SUBHEAD, BODY COPY.

Strip out any non-copy or non-label wording. Give your copy another look-through after formatting; leaving old versions of lines or other mistakes is very easy to accidentally do. Be sure, too, to pull out any necessary notes and either put them in comments or save them for discussing elsewhere.

CHAPTER 12

EDIT LIKE A PRO

At least 50 percent of the work for every copywriting project is editing. You'll work hard to get your best ideas down and phrase them the best you can, but the simple truth is that you'll get the best result by refining that first draft.

If anything, this should make writing copy a bit easier. You don't have to be perfect! Your first draft is just that, and as a draft, it is your first attempt at using everything you've learned to craft an effective message. Editing allows you to revisit the project and evaluate and improve what you've done.

Even better, there's nothing magical about the editing process that you haven't already heard about. You'll review your work and compare what you've written to the foundational principles you've learned in this book. The difference, though, is that because you already have a draft finished, you'll be able to view what you've done through much more objective eyes.

Strategy Session

You've gotten through this much of the book so you already know that each project needs to start with a thoroughly written creative brief (see page 52) and a messaging outline (see page 26) based on that brief. Check and check.

After that, you'll flesh out that outline by writing copy based on the key points of the brief (see page 63), what you know about the target audience (see page 36), and the brand's voice (see page 102). And then?

You walk away.

Truly. At this stage of the game, the best thing you can do for your copywriting project is get some distance. Go for a walk, do some laundry, take a nap—anything to give your brain an adequate rest. You need to give your conscious mind a break. This will help you come back to your copy with fresh eyes and a more objective perspective.

When you're ready to sit back down to do your editing, do your best to imagine that this isn't your own copy. Approach the words as if you're just evaluating the writing to see how what you're reviewing measures up, and look for any opportunities for improvement.

Pull out your creative brief for reference. Then, ask yourself each of these questions about the copy you're editing—and think honestly and carefully about the answers:

- Does this copy hit the creative brief's key points?

- Are these words the target audience would use?

- Are there any extraneous words?

- Are there any extraneous lines—or even paragraphs?

- Are the paragraphs long?

- Are the sentences long?

- Is the benefit in the headline?

- Does the messaging hook the reader?

- Does the copy stay focused and keep the reader's attention?

- Do the messages lead to the CTA?

- Is the CTA strong and clear?

Any instances where your copy doesn't quite measure up (or could be improved on) are opportunities for editing.

And if you have a lot of changes to make based on this evaluation? Great! A need for editing is not an opportunity to beat yourself up or cut yourself down; rather, you can do even better work. Perfection is impossible, but incremental improvements in your copy will lead to incremental improvements in its effectiveness.

Case in Point

Writing like we're all still in English class is one of the hardest habits for new copywriters to break but is also one of the most important. Get used to breaking up sentences and paragraphs. Write in the voice of the brand, and don't be afraid to write like people speak.

When doing a website redesign, XYZ Skincare, Inc. called in a copywriter to help. The information in the old website was correct and compelling, but people weren't reading their copy, and worse, people who did weren't understanding or retaining the information. The copywriter suspected some serious editing was in order.

This is some of the original copy on the XYZ website:

XYZ solution is an award-winning, dermatologist-recommended, completely game-changing serum and spot concealer in one that instantly corrects hyperpigmentation with buildable concealer for a fresh, natural look and then treats spots with a highly effective, proprietary 5 percent retinol solution so that dark spots are dramatically faded with every use!

The copywriter identified that the paragraph was too long and the sentence was densely packed with too much information. At the same time, the copywriter knew that the client didn't want to drastically change the language.

To keep the copy focused on the most important information, make the copy easier to read, and make the information more accessible—while still retaining much of the same language—the copywriter recommended:

Cover and treat hyperpigmentation at the same time!

XYZ delivers instant results with a buildable concealer for a fresh, natural look. Meanwhile, its proprietary 5 percent retinol solution dramatically fades dark spots with every use.

Award-winning. Dermatologist-recommended. Game-changing.

KEEP IN MIND

Editing your own work can be a challenge, but it's worth the work. Here are a few points to keep in mind:

Key Takeaways

Editing is copywriting. You won't stumble onto perfection in your first draft. Editing is where you refine and shine.

Editing your work requires fresh eyes. Switching from writing to editing is very hard. You'll get much better results if you give your brain a break in between tasks.

Be your own toughest creative director. A copywriter often works with a creative director to get insightful, expert feedback—as well as unbiased, unemotional feedback. Be nice to yourself, but be tough on your work.

Action Items

Give your brain a break. Once you're done writing, get up and walk away. Give yourself anywhere from a few hours to a full day to process what you've done and get a fresh perspective.

Be ruthless—take out what shouldn't be there. Be gentle with yourself but ruthless with your copy. If a word, line, or even paragraph distracts from your message, cut out the offender.

Polish what should stay. This work might mean cutting extraneous words or rephrasing or swapping out words to better connect with the target audience.

CHAPTER 13

TRAIN YOUR BRAIN FOR COPY

From billboards, newspaper ads, and direct mail to emails, websites, banner ads, and so much more, we're swimming in a world of copy. In fact, I'd bet you can find some kind of copy within about three feet of where you're sitting right now. Back cover or jacket copy on a book? Check. Packaging on a new purchase? Check. Even taglines on branded T-shirts. All copy.

Most of us, though, have learned to ignore the copy around us. Even worse for you as a copywriter, you likely don't notice even when copy *does* work and catches your attention. Well, your days of copy oblivion are over.

One of the best ways to improve your copywriting skills is to make use of the copy that's already out there in the world, which is exactly what this chapter teaches.

A word of warning: Many would-be copywriters skip this step. They'd rather just dig in and get to writing. But if you truly want to craft the best copy you can and become the most adept and skilled copywriter you can be, this strategy is essential.

Imagine a film director who never watched movies. A novelist who never read books. An electrician who never turned on the lights. (Okay, that's a stretch, but you get where I'm going.) Truly skilled people are interested in their craft. So get interested in the copy around you.

Strategy Session

Just by starting to take note of the copy around you, you'll already be making major strides in your copywriting skills. But instead of just strides, wouldn't you rather make leaps and bounds?

Here's a three-step approach to hone your observational, analytical, and writing skills. Because copy is everywhere, you can try this approach anywhere: in the supermarket checkout line, in the waiting room at the dentist's, while stuck in traffic. Once this approach becomes a habit, you'll know you're on the road to mastery.

STEP ONE: NOTICE

Noticing is harder than you may think. You're likely so used to scrolling past ads online or automatically tossing out ads in your mail that not reading copy has become a habit. If you have trouble reminding yourself to stop and look for copy, set reminders on your phone to go off a few times throughout the day. Then, whatever you're doing when the alarm rings, look for any copy that happens to be nearby and *read the words*.

Don't automatically delete emails from companies and organizations anymore. (Or, at least, not every single one.) Don't scroll past sponsored Instagram ads. Don't flip past ads in magazines. Stop and read instead.

STEP TWO: EVALUATE

Once you've developed a habit to stop, notice, and read the copy around you, take the exercise to the next level. For each piece of copy you read, evaluate the likelihood of the copy's effectiveness.

Apply the foundational principles you've already learned in this book and see if that copy lives up to what you've learned. Ask yourself if the benefit to the consumer is clear. Is the CTA straightforward? Do the words speak to the target audience? Is the messaging likely to draw in the target and keep them interested? Applying all of these and the other copywriting essentials will yield a treasure trove of insight.

Be sure not to just settle for "I like the copy" or "I don't like the copy." Sometimes copy we "like" (rhyming, funny, entertaining) doesn't actually adhere to the tenets of good copy. And if the words don't do what's needed, the copy is worthless.

So, is the copy effective? If so, why? Less than effective? If so, why? Explain to yourself what makes the copy good or why improvement is called for.

STEP THREE: REWRITE

When you come across a piece of copy that doesn't do the job, take the situation as a challenge.

You've made a pretty good guess at what you think the benefit should be, who the target audience likely is, and what action the advertiser wants them to take. So with all of that information on hand, try making this particular piece of copy more effective by rewriting. What didn't work in the real version? Fix the copy in yours. You don't have to make what you create look like the original piece, just make a copy doc. The value is in the copy itself.

Do you have to do this exercise for every single subpar piece of copy you come across? Of course not. But if you make this effort for even a small fraction of the pieces you read, you'll make tremendous progress in your evaluation, writing, and editing skills.

So few people actually try correcting what they come across . . . which is precisely why I am challenging you to be one of the few who does.

Case in Point

Where should you be looking for copy? Everywhere! Remember, copy is any writing with the goal of persuading people or getting them to take action (whereas content is writing designed to educate, entertain, or inspire, or any combination of all three).

In case you're still at a bit of a loss, here's a (by no means exhaustive!) list of places to look for copy:

- Instagram ads—in feeds, in stories, etc.
- Facebook ads
- Google ads
- Websites
- Nonprofit donation request letters
- Direct mail postcards and letters
- Emails
- Product descriptions (Amazon, apps, podcasts, etc.)
- LinkedIn profile bios
- Flyers
- Menus
- Billboards
- Newspaper or magazine ads
- Product packaging
- Book jackets or back covers

There are all kinds of everyday communications that people don't even realize is copy. An email to a boss asking for a few days off is trying to persuade that boss to grant the request. A dating profile is trying to persuade potential dates to get in touch. A PTA memo about a bake sale is trying to persuade people to volunteer or purchase baked goods.

Copy is all around you. Start keeping your eyes out.

Love may have been all around Mary Tyler Moore (Anyone? Classic sitcom theme song? Am I getting punchy while writing this book and will my editor take this out?), but copy is all around *us*. The sooner you start using all of that to your advantage, the sooner you'll turn the world on with your ~~smile~~ copywriting skills.

Key Takeaways

Copy is all around you. Really: from the message on an envelope that says "Time-sensitive offer inside" to the email about a sale at your favorite store. Copy is everywhere.

Some copy is good, some is not so good. Just like anything else, there's a sliding scale of quality for the copy out there. You get to discern which pieces do their jobs and which don't.

If the copy is not doing the job, it's not good. Copy that doesn't live up to the principles you've learned isn't going to have the impact the writer and brand intended.

Action Items

Start noticing. Train yourself to turn off your autopilot and actually notice the copy you come across each day. Having a hard time? Set alarms to remind yourself.

Start analyzing. Compare the copy you see to the principles you've learned. What works? What doesn't? And, most important, why?

Rewrite. Once you know why something doesn't work in a copy piece, rework to get to a better version.

CHAPTER 14

LEARN TO LOVE YOUR DATA

R eady for another big difference between copywriting and other forms of writing? In copywriting, success is measurable. Instead of just sending copy out into the world and hoping the goals are met, companies and organizations can look at specific data sets (metrics) to actually measure what the copy does.

I know the idea of measuring your work might make you uncomfortable, but trust me, a data set is our friend. When we're writing copy, we're certainly doing the best work we can but people are unpredictable.

Data lets you know whether your copy is actually moving people to take action and to what degree. You'll see in the next chapter (page 95) how data enables you to make your copy more effective.

If you are both a business owner and your own copywriter, you'll have access to these data points through the software you use to run your email and build your website and landing pages. If you're writing for someone else, you may have to ask them to dig into their metrics and get you the relevant numbers. Either way, these results—the data points you'll learn about as you read this chapter—will give you simple, straightforward insight into the performance of your copy.

Strategy Session

Data analysts will balk at the list I'm about to give you—there are many, many more data points to explore—but most relevant for copywriters are the metrics that reveal the most about how their copy performs.

For the metrics, I'll explain what each is, what each demonstrates, where to find each, and where general industry benchmarks fall so that you can begin to get a sense of how you're doing. Bear in mind, though, that benchmarks are just numbers to be aware of—they can be affected by a lot of factors and benchmarks of success for your particular industry may be higher or lower.

The most important metrics are *your* numbers because once you know how your copy is performing, you can adjust for improvement. You learned a bit about these metrics in chapter 2 (see page 11), though I'll also provide a little definition refresher. Now I'll go through how to read them.

OPEN RATE

What open rate is: The percentage of people who opened an email out of all who received the message. The open rate demonstrates the power of the brand sending the email but, much more significantly, reflects the effectiveness of the subject line, the only copy a recipient sees until an email is opened.

Where to find open rate: Check the data sets provided by your email service provider (the company you use to send your email). The data will include the open rate for each email you've sent.

Benchmark: Your open rate should be between 15 percent and 25 percent, though the first email you send after a subscriber opts in tends to skew a lot higher, sometimes as high as 50 or 60 percent. What a great opportunity to get important messages in front of your target audience, right?

CLICK-THROUGH RATE

What click-through rate is: The percentage of people who take the call to action you've given them and click on a link you've provided out of all of who see the CTA. Click-through rate can refer to people clicking a link on a website or landing page, in an email, or on an ad. Because the user is taking this step (or not), the data will reflect the effectiveness of the copy on that website, landing page, email, or ad.

Where to find the click-through rate: Because click-through rates can apply to a few different types of messaging, there will be different places to find this metric for each type of project. For websites and landing pages, look at your website analytics software or, if you use special software to build landing pages, look there. Your email service provider will have information about click-through rates for each email, and the ad platform you're using (Facebook, Instagram, Google, etc.) will have data about the click-through rates for your ads.

Benchmark: This number will vary wildly across the type of medium. For Facebook ads for example, the benchmark is around 1 to 2 percent. For email, you'll want to see more like 2.5 percent. For a website or landing page, unfortunately, giving a benchmark is a little hard because the number will depend on the type of pages, where people are going, and the audience.

CONVERSION RATE

What conversion rate is: Technically speaking, conversion rate is the percentage of people who "convert" from one type of interaction with you to another. Most commonly you'll hear conversion rate referenced in regard to purchases or subscribers: A person "converts" from someone who was not a purchaser to someone who is, or from someone who was not a subscriber to someone who is. With purchasers, the conversion rate refers to the percentage of people who purchased after seeing your sales message. With subscribers, conversion rate is the percentage of people who opted-in (subscribed) after seeing your opt-in message. (Conversion rates for opt-ins are also often called "opt-in rates." Same thing.)

Where to find conversion rate data: Finding the stats related to conversion rate can get a little tricky because you may have to compare data from different sources to come up with the number. For example, you may get the number of people who saw your sales page from your landing page software, whereas to see the percentage of people who actually made a purchase, you'll need to go to your sales software. Your email service provider may be able to directly give you your opt-in rate or if you use a different software to build out the forms on your site, that software may tell you. So you *might* have to do a little digging to get a conversion rate but doing so is worth the effort because this metric is crucial.

Benchmark: Because there are wildly different types of conversion rates, there are also wildly different types of benchmarks. Ballpark-wise, a good purchase conversion rate (purchase rate) is 2 percent. A good subscriber conversion rate (opt-in rate) is between 5 percent and 15 percent.

Case in Point

A retailer of high-end men's blue-blocker sunglasses wasn't seeing the results he was hoping for from his ad campaign. He was running ads on Facebook and spending a solid amount each day, but the results in sales just weren't happening.

His ad linked to an opt-in page for people to sign up for emails. From there, the subscriber got a series of emails about the product that led to the sales page. Because there were so many moving pieces to this campaign, he was confused about where to look to evaluate the situation.

A marketing friend of his gave him this checklist to help him understand where his campaign was underperforming—and where his opportunities lay.

If click-through on the ad is low, the ad needs improvement. If the ad copy isn't doing the job, people won't click.

If click-through on the ad is good but the opt-in rate is low, the opt-in page needs improvement. If the opt-in page isn't compelling, people won't click to join the email list.

If click-through on the ad is good, the opt-in rate is good, but the opening rate on emails is low, the subject lines need improvement. If the subject line isn't effective, no one will open the email.

If click-through on the ad is good, the opt-in rate is good, the opening rate on email is good, but the click-through in the email is low, the copy in the body of the email needs improvement. If the email copy doesn't inspire people to learn more, they won't click.

If all of the above are good, but the purchase rate on the sales page is low, the sales page needs improvement. If the sales page doesn't drive people to purchase, they won't.

Metrics are incredibly useful but can also be overwhelming. Stay focused on the data that matters most to you and your business and track how your copy is performing.

Key Takeaways

Data sets are the best indicators of how your copy is actually performing. Even better, they give you clear guidance about where you can improve.

Track your data over time. Looking at your data once can be very informative, but you'll learn even more if you look at the numbers regularly and keep track of what's happening. This will let you spot downward (or upward!) changes and deal with them as needed.

Don't jump to conclusions. If something isn't performing the way you'd expect, don't assume you need to make changes to every customer touch point. Dig into your data to figure out exactly where the problem is.

Action Items

Gather your data sources. Make sure you have access to analytics on your website, landing page software, email service provider, ad platforms, and sales software.

Understand which data points mean what. Not all data is created equal, and some will have much greater impact than others. Make sure you understand your numbers before you draw any conclusions.

Examine each part of the customer journey separately. You certainly can look at the results of a multi-part campaign as a whole but break down each part and look at the metrics to understand where things are underperforming—and where you can improve.

CHAPTER 15

TEST YOUR COPY AND MAKE SMART ADJUSTMENTS

Whereas you'll always strive to do your best work and put your best foot forward with your copywriting, the people who read what you write are unpredictable. Knowing exactly *what* is going to resonate best with whom at any given time is impossible.

Data helps you learn what's working and what's not, and testing helps you find ways to improve. Pitting two CTA lines against each other, for example, in a valid and properly structured test (more on how in a sec, see page 97) will help you learn which one encourages people to take action and which falls flat. And with this information, you can go with the more effective line.

The concept of "testing" your work can feel intimidating for copywriters. If so, think of the process more as measurement than performing a test. No one expects you to be perfect nor to read minds. (Also important is remembering *you* are not your copy!) Testing is simply measuring two elements of your copywriting against each other to see which resonates more with the reader.

Testing lets you take what you know, combine the results with data, and come up with the solution with the highest impact.

Strategy Session

This session addresses a few different types of testing to help determine which one you should (likely) opt for, what to test, and how to go about the process. Phew! Ready?

TYPES OF TESTS

Somewhere an analyst is shaking their fist at me, but I'm going to keep things simple. For our purposes here, there are really two types of testing: A/B testing and multivariate testing.

A/B testing means pitting two options against each other—an A version and a B version—both presented to the same kind of audience in the same way. For example, you might set up an A/B test to try out two different versions of a landing page, with version A automatically shown to half of the page visitors and version B shown to the other half. The page that shows the highest click-through rate (or opt-in rate or whatever you're measuring) is the winner. With this information, you then show the winning page to *all* users.

The most common way to do A/B testing is to test *one* single difference. For example, version A might have one headline and version B a different one—but everything else stays the same. This way, you know that any difference in results is attributable to the headline.

Multivariate testing means you're testing a bunch of different elements all at once. This process makes tracking much harder than in A/B testing and therefore much harder to know which difference created which result.

If you haven't guessed by now, sticking with A/B testing is much easier and more effective. And you'll be surprised how one little tweak to a headline, CTA, subject line, or some other piece of copy can have a huge impact on your results.

WHAT TO TEST

Here's a roundup of the easiest elements to test, which, fortunately, are also likely to have the highest impact. Remember, you're testing these elements one at a time! Find a winner and *then* move on to your next test. Also, you don't have to test every single one.

- Headlines
- Subject lines
- Body copy
- Calls to action
- Opt-ins (the copy asking people to opt-in OR the actual opt-in reward itself)
- Images (yes, this category is out of the copy purview but is still a testing option)

HOW TO TEST

The best and easiest way to test something is to make use of technology. Your email service provider likely makes testing your subject lines and email copy very easy, whereas your landing page software is where you go to test changes to your landing pages. Some software specifically made for testing is also available and is much more accurate than trying to test your copy manually. To find the software, start by searching for "A/B testing software."

The software will automatically break your traffic into two equal groups, will show both groups the tests, and will record the results. Using technology is, hands down, the better way to go.

Can you test on your own in a pinch? Yes. For example, if you have an automated email that goes out, you might send one subject line for two weeks and then switch to a different subject line for another two weeks and see which resulted in a better open rate. This option isn't really a completely valid test because there are all kinds of factors that could change for your audience in those two different two-week periods. But if you don't have the proper software for testing, following this plan is better than nothing.

Case in Point

I hope testing sounds more manageable and doable now than before you read this section, but maybe you're still thinking that you might not bother. Let's look at some numbers to see if I can convince you.

Suppose your normal email opt-in rate is 30 percent and your normal sales conversion percent from subscribers (the percentage out of all your subscribers that purchases) is 3 percent on a $500 product.

And let's say you change your opt-in language and get a 3 percent increase in subscribers—from 30 percent to 33 percent. Here's how that breaks out over a year:

Pre–Opt-In Change: 10,000 visitors monthly → 3,000 subscribers → 90 purchasers → $45,000 monthly → $540,000 yearly

Post–Opt-In Change: 10,000 visitors monthly → 3,300 subscribers → 99 purchasers → $49,500 monthly → $594,000 yearly

This difference represents an extra $54,000 in a year from just ONE little change in your opt-in copy!

Then, what if you tested and changed your sales page headline and doing so increased your sales conversion rate from 3 to 4 percent. One little percent—what can that do?

Well, your purchasers would increase from 99 to 132 each month, your revenue would increase from $49,500 to $66,000 each month, and your yearly revenue would increase to $792,000.

Two little tests and changes take you from grossing $540,000 to $792,000 per year. I'd say those tests were worth the effort, wouldn't you?

Obviously, not every test is going to work and not every change will have drastic results. But this scenario illustrates why testing is so important: You can't possibly know the outcome until you try.

KEEP IN MIND

Testing provides the opportunity to make our copywriting better, more effective, and more resonant with our target audience.

Key Takeaways

Testing is your friend. Testing can have massive positive impacts on your results so learn to like the testing process or even—dare I say?—love it!

Test everything you can. Nothing is off-limits. Make an orderly testing plan so you don't drive yourself nuts but do at least test the major elements of your copy.

Test one element at a time (A/B testing). When you test a bunch of things at once (multivariate testing), you can't know which change had the impact. Organize so you're only testing one key element per test.

Action Items

Identify high-impact copy for testing. Evaluate your audience touch points and figure out which pieces of copy could have the most impact on your business if they were improved.

Write two or three variations (that still meet your creative brief). Pull out your brief to help you write a few copy versions for testing that still meet all your brand and business objectives.

Test in the same conditions. Software automates the process of showing different versions to your audience. With software, you'll have the most reliable results.

PART THREE

Specific Copywriting Strategies

With the solid foundation of the core principles of copywriting now under your belt, this part teaches you how to use these principles to write specific types of copy.

Of course, I couldn't include how to write *all* types of copy in this book. But we'll cover the sorts you're most likely to need as well as tips to guide you when tasked with writing copy for any medium.

CHAPTER 16

CREATING A BRAND VOICE AND TONE GUIDE

Just like people, brands have distinct voices and styles of "speaking." Some brands are quirky and funny, some are straightforward and stoic, and some are friendly and open. (And that's just a few examples.)

If a person we know were to suddenly start speaking in a different tone or style than usual, we would feel unsettled. The same basic idea applies when a brand's voice changes from one copy piece to another; consumers find the change off-putting. Establishing—and sticking with—a consistent voice and tone helps the target audience learn to like and trust the brand.

A "tone guide" documents the personality of the brand, including the brand voice, but goes deeper by identifying words or phrases a brand would and wouldn't use. This resource will be essential to guide you as you write copy but also invaluable if you ever hire a copywriter to work for you.

This next session focuses on how to make your own tone guide.

Strategy Session

A quick note before we begin: If you're writing for someone else's company, it may already have an established and documented brand voice and tone guide. If so, great! Often, though, companies have a general voice and a communication style . . . but these choices have never been clearly thought through and documented. Going through this exercise will help you keep that existing voice and tone consistent going forward—and ensure that you're writing in a way that melds with copy that's already out there.

BRAND VOICE

Let's start out by establishing a brand voice. You might do this practice for your own business or, if you want, as an exercise for any existing brand you choose. Here are the steps to follow:

Step #1: If this brand were a person, how would you describe them? Write down a description that's as detailed as possible. "Nice" isn't specific enough to be helpful when you're writing, but "friendly" or "supportive" would be.

Step #2: Review your description and think through each word to make sure what you've come up with *truly* fits the brand. For example, "playful" and "fun" are similar, but there's still a big difference between them. Same for "forceful" and "bold." Grab a thesaurus (okay, okay—find one online) and explore a bit to make sure you hit on the exact right words.

Step #3: Be sure you're describing the brand's *voice* not the brand's products or services. The McDonald's voice is youthful, fun, and energetic. But is the voice fast? No—the food service it provides is fast but not the brand.

Step #4: Edit your description, narrowing to a list of five (or so) of the best descriptors. These descriptors should be present in all of the brand's major pieces of messaging, so choosing more than five sets you up for an unnecessary challenge when copywriting. These final five descriptors are your brand's voice.

TONE GUIDE

Now, let's talk about the tone guide. This resource covers the words or phrases a brand would—or definitely would *not*—use.

Knowing what you know about the brand, what words would it be likely to say? If this brand has an established history, what words does it regularly use? (That are on brand!)

What words would it NOT use?

Repeat this exercise ("would use" versus "wouldn't use") with regard to phrases.

Here's a quick example:

- McDonald's would say things that sound tasty like "A sizzling all-beef patty."

- McDonald's would NOT say things that sound too high-end or expensive, like "The finest ground sirloin available on the market."

Put your brand voice notes and your tone guide together in a document and refer to it regularly when you write—and when you edit!—to make sure your copywriting is consistent with the rest of the brand's marketing.

Case in Point

Let's explore how the brand voice plays out in two well-known brands. A quick note: Brands do, periodically, update or change their brand voices. Doing so is a major undertaking and is usually part of a full "rebranding initiative." What I've written here is current as of this book's publication. Also, there's no perfect or iron-clad description of a particular brand—at least, from the outside; the brand may have one for itself.

The Kate Spade brand voice: Kate Spade is a fashion and lifestyle brand that sells handbags, shoes, clothing, and some housewares, all geared toward women. The brand is not inexpensive, so the voice is somewhat aspirational. At the same time, however, the brand marketers make the brand seem accessible. The brand voice for Kate Spade is confident, clever, intelligent, and youthful (but not young). The copy is insightful and inspirational but is never snobby or overly monied.

The GoDaddy brand voice: GoDaddy is primarily a web hosting service but provides other internet services like email and website building. The brand voice for GoDaddy is bold, urgent, and fresh. The copy is straightforward and definitely a little bit techy. The voice may push the boundaries a bit but is never overtly rude or dismissive and never overly "masculine."

The trick to writing a brand voice is that you have to be sure not to alienate any members of your target audience. GoDaddy, for example, is a consumer brand that sells to all genders so whereas it can make the choice to sound a little bit more like a "guy," it has to be very careful not to push too far in that direction.

The brand voice is how the brand sounds to the target audience, which will have a major impact on how the brand is perceived.

Key Takeaways

A brand should sound consistent in all copy. Though some pieces of copy will be so short there won't be much opportunity to infuse a lot of voice, all copy from a brand should sound like that brand.

A brand voice is how a brand sounds. The voice is the personality of a brand and the traits that the personality display through the copy.

A tone guide is a write-up of the voice as well as a document of word and phrase usage. Voice is the *way* a brand speaks, including the common (or plausible) words and phrases it uses.

Action Items

Evaluate and describe your brand as you would a person. Take some time to immerse yourself in the brand and think carefully about its traits. Be specific.

Decide which words and phrases the brand would use—and which wouldn't be appropriate. Based on what you know about the voice and the brand, make note of what the brand has "said" (or is likely to "say") and what it hasn't and definitely wouldn't.

Put your thoughts together in one doc to refer to regularly. Use this document to inspire you as you begin writing and then rely on what's there to guide you as you begin editing.

CHAPTER 17

WRITING EMAILS

I n spite of some tech guy announcing that "email is dead" every few months, I can assure you that not only is email very much alive and kicking, this type of communication is still one of the most effective and powerful means of reaching a target audience.

Think for a sec: Your email list is a group of people who actively made the choice to subscribe to you because they're so interested in or excited by what you have to offer. Every email message, then, is a very powerful opportunity.

This chapter explores the different styles of email copywriting and offers the most effective ways to wield them.

Strategy Session

A quick reminder: Always start with a creative brief (see chapter 6, page 52). I've spared you the monotony of repeating this directive in each strategy session, but remember that the creative brief organizes the project at the outset, gives you a good place to start from, and is a guide to evaluate (and edit) what you've written. 'Nuff said.

Generally speaking (but admittedly a bit oversimplified), there are two types of email you'll be writing: letter-style and promotional. Keeping these two types of emails in mind is a good way to start.

Letter-style emails tend to be text-only emails sent by small companies or solopreneurs, written as if they're actually coming from the owner or a member of the team. They're typically used to build a strong rapport with the recipient.

Promotional emails are focused on a specific promotion (a sale, giveaway, special announcement, etc.), and they usually include images and relatively little copy. Think of the emails you receive from e-commerce companies.

Could there be some overlap and intermingling of the styles? Absolutely. Remember, I'm oversimplifying to give you a good place to start. But before we even get into the emails themselves, we need to talk about the single most important part of an email: the subject line.

Why is this one element so important? Well, if the subject line doesn't catch the recipient's attention and get them to open the email, the rest of the email is completely irrelevant.

There are two ways to go with the subject line: Either write to the benefit of the email or pique your reader's curiosity.

You're already a pro at identifying and writing to a benefit (and if you're feeling less than pro-level, revisit chapters 5 and 6). And you're already a pro at piquing interest as well (see chapter 7, page 54). Just like when crafting any other hook, your email subject line should be genuinely interesting and actually relate to the content of the email.

Let's break down the best practices for your email copywriting.

SUBJECT LINE DOS AND DON'TS

- **Do** put the most important words at the beginning of the line so they don't get cut off.

- **Do** use a snippet or pre-header to add more details and support your subject line (if your email service provider gives you the option).

- **Don't** try to find the "perfect character count." Just write the best line you can.

- **Don't** settle with just one subject line: Test, test, test! (See chapter 15 page 95.)

PROMO EMAIL DOS AND DON'TS

- **Do** keep the message concise: Stick to a headline, a subhead (if needed), body copy (if needed) and a call to action (CTA).

- **Don't** forget your CTA! You'd be surprised how many promo emails do.

- **Don't** stray from your brand voice.

LETTER-STYLE EMAIL DOS AND DON'TS

- **Do** be sure to outline your messaging first.

- **Do** include messages leading your reader to the inevitability of taking the action spelled out in your CTA.

- **Do** consider making your tone feel more personal, because you're building a relationship—think of writing to a close friend.

- **Don't** forget to start with a hook.

- **Don't** think that letter-style emails don't need a CTA! Sometimes you may be directing people to a sales page or content, or you may just be instructing "keep your eyes on your inbox" for the next email.

Case in Point

How do you decide which kind of email to send? Here's how that question shakes out for a few types of businesses:

Business: Jim's Gem Jam, a jewelry designer
Purpose of Emails: Highlight new products weekly
This jewelry maker is aiming to promote (and sell) his newest item each week. Because this message is promotional and concise and is highly focused on imagery, he opts for a promo-style email.

Business: The Pennyface Group, an investments advisor
Purpose of Emails: Dissect and discuss individual stocks
This investment advisor wants to send out weekly emails in which she gives an analysis of popular stocks and advises whether her clients should consider investing. Because the messages are longer and more in-depth, she opted for text-only, letter-style emails.

Business: Susan Shoots, a branding photographer
Purpose of Emails: Inspire people to book photography sessions
This branding photographer wanted to demonstrate her expertise but, unfortunately, initially went about her approach the wrong way. She began with long, letter-style emails explaining the technical aspects of her photo shoot setups. These messages would have been great for a target of other photographers but not so great for her actual target audience of people interested in the end result, not in the process.
When she switches to promo-style emails full of great photos and concise, compelling copy encouraging them to book sessions, her schedule is soon full of new assignments.

Bottom line: Evaluate each of your emails individually to determine which style makes the most sense. *Then* begin filling out your creative brief and outlining your message.

Emails should be a key marketing tactic for any business or organization—no matter how big or small. Here are a few essentials to ensure that your emails stay on track.

Key Takeaways

Most emails will be either letter-style or promo-style. Your message (and brand) will dictate which one you should choose.

The subject line is your most important piece of copy. Even if you write the best email body copy in the world, no one will ever see what you've written if your subject line doesn't entice them to open the message!

Remember to structure your email so that your CTA is inevitable. Whether you're writing a promo- or letter-style email, the copy should lead directly to your CTA.

Action Items

Decide which type of email to write. Though I'm oversimplifying, most of your emails are going to fall into either the letter-style or promo-style camp.

Write several versions of your subject line. Your subject line is crucial so spend some serious time on this element—and write a couple of different versions to test them.

Outline your messaging and then fill in the outline. Don't get overwhelmed by how much messaging can go in an email (letter-style emails, especially). Start with your outline and go from there.

CHAPTER 18

CRAFTING EMAIL FUNNELS

Email funnels are about conversion. The "funnel" is actually a series of carefully crafted, automated emails that lead your reader from one experience (say, being just newly aware of your brand) to another state (ready to purchase!). They are an incredibly effective tool for guiding people along the customer journey.

Email funnels allow you to build a relationship, on autopilot, with your prospective customers. By carefully crafting the messages in these emails, you can build the essential "know, like, and trust factor" in your readers' minds and cultivate a genuine connection with them.

Though not every type of company or organization uses email funnels, I can't think of any that wouldn't benefit from at least testing them. Instead of trying to get a subscriber to take a major action (like make a purchase) in just one email, funnels give you the opportunity to connect with your target over a series of messages, nurturing the relationship so that they're finally ready to take that action.

Strategy Session

The first step in creating your email funnel is to identify what kind of relationship an audience has with you now versus where you want them to go. Are you launching a new product to people already on your list who are familiar with you and trying to get them to buy? Or are you sending your messages to people who have just subscribed to your list in order to build your relationship with them to get them to buy your lowest-priced item?

Once you determine the target audience (which could very well be a smaller segment of your entire audience), your next step is to think about what messages you want to convey. Here are a few questions to help you get started:

- Why do people need what you have to offer?

- Why are people afraid to purchase what you have to offer? What objections do they have?

- Why should people purchase from you instead of any of your competitors?

- What are some little-known facts about your product, service, or field that people should know?

- Do you have any stories about people who have purchased your product or service and were pleased? What was their life like before your product or service? What about after?

- What's your story? How did you decide to start offering this product or service?

- What are common misconceptions about your product, service, or industry?

- What are the benefits of using your product or service? What are the best possible results?

- Do you have any testimonials about your business, product, or service?

- What blog posts, videos, or other resources do you have that are especially useful to prospective customers? Check and see which of your posts, videos, and other materials have gotten the most comments or the most likes or shares on social media. People interact with things they like!

Once you've answered these questions and amassed your resources, your next step is to organize your messages. Keep these points in mind:

Take it slow. Remember, you're gently taking people down a path from (potentially) knowing nothing about you and your product or service to, eventually, wanting to purchase from you. This process has to be gradual and has to gel with the way people are thinking as they interact with you and your messages.

If they've just joined your list and don't know much about you or your product or service, sending them glowing testimonials about you right away may not make sense. They haven't even decided if what you offer might make sense for them.

Create a flow. Throughout your funnel, each email should naturally flow into the next. Creating this flow is what editing is for! This process is going to take some thinking, some moving of pieces around, and some revising. But editing is an incredibly important part of the process, so give yourself time.

Let them know. Get creative, but always, above all else, think of providing value to the people you're writing to. They'll stick with your funnel, keep reading your emails, and develop an affinity for you and your business if you make those emails worthwhile and beneficial for them. Be sure that they know how they'll benefit from your messages.

Show them where to go. And, of course, you want to structure your funnel so that taking the final action is practically a no-brainer (similar to the approach to CTAs, see page 69). You need to give them the right messages and information, overcome their objections, demonstrate the value of your offer (and, if applicable, of you and your company), and connect with what your audience wants and needs.

Follow the workflow. As with any copy project, start with a creative brief for your funnel, create an outline, fill in your messages, and then write each email. When you review them, look at them individually, but also weigh their impact together. Shine and refine as needed!

Rely on a pro. A note on technology: To create an email funnel, you'll need a professional email service provider—your standard Gmail won't cut it. (And no company should be sending professional emails from a personal Gmail anyway!) Companies like Constant Contact, MailChimp, and others make setting up your funnel easy and, even better, have plenty of tutorials to guide you, and they offer excellent customer service if needed.

Case in Point

A women's supplements company was planning its first email funnel. Its plan was to get people on their list via a website quiz that would require people to opt-in to get the results. It wanted to take people from this first discovery of the brand to wanting to purchase a sample pack of their special pre- and probiotic supplement.

The company knew it would have to deliver the results of the quiz, address why its supplement is so essential to women's health, differentiate itself from the competition, share customer success stories, overcome the "I can get something like this in my local drug store" objection, overcome the price objection, *and* ask the subscriber to make a purchase.

This is how the company decided to structure its funnel:

Email 1: Welcome, quiz result delivery. CTA: Watch a video about the quiz results.

Email 2: Education about product effectiveness. CTA: Click to view a comparison chart of their product versus competitors.

Email 3: Client success story #1. CTA: Watch video testimonial.

Email 4: Education about difference between product and drug store options. CTA: Watch in-box for special offer.

Email 5: Special first-time purchase discount. CTA: Buy now.

Email 6: Client success stories #2, time running out to use discount. CTA: Buy now.

Email 7: Client success story #3, last chance to use discount. CTA: Buy now.

The company also set up rules so that if subscribers purchased the product, they would leave this welcome funnel and enter a post-sample-purchase funnel. That funnel then encouraged them to try the product, track their results, share their results, and purchase a full subscription for the product.

An email funnel is a powerfully effective way to build a genuine relationship with your audience and guide them toward the actions you want them to take.

Key Takeaways

A funnel takes a reader from one state to another. No matter where a reader is on the customer journey, your funnel can help gently guide them to the next step—or through the next several steps.

A funnel should unfold over several days. Plan to send your emails at a one-a-day, or even one-every-other day, rate. And don't worry too much about unsubscribes—if they don't want what you've got, let 'em go!

An email funnel builds the know, like, and trust factors. A big part of creating a relationship with your subscriber is letting them gradually get to know you and helping them gradually learn to trust your expertise.

Action Items

Identify where they are and where you want to take them. Before you start writing, figure out exactly where your email subscriber is on their customer journey (just heard of you, been following you but hasn't bought, etc.) and what action you'd like them to take at the end of the funnel.

Identify what the subscriber will need to know to take your desired action. Plan out your messaging to convey any key information, share success stories, and overcome any objections they might have to taking the action.

Organize your messages to make that action a no-brainer. Plan the order of your emails to lead naturally from one to the next, with the ultimate, inevitable outcome of taking the action at the end of your funnel.

CHAPTER 19

WRITING WEBSITES

People think of a business or organization's website as its definitive resource. They go to the website when they want to know more, they go to the website when they want to make a purchase, they go to the website when they want to determine if they can trust the company. A website must serve a lot of different purposes for a lot of different people—and all must be done very well.

But just as every business is different, every website is different, has different purposes, and serves different target audiences. This section dives into how to approach this big project, reviews the factors to consider when planning, and takes you through ways to get down to work.

Strategy Session

I promised I wouldn't remind you to use a creative brief in each chapter, but the advice bears repeating for this topic. And here's the thing: When writing a website, you want to use a creative brief in two ways.

Step one is to develop a creative brief for the entire site to help you identify a few key factors. Create the full brief but first consider these essential points:

- What is the purpose of the website as a whole? What is the ultimate desired outcome?

- Who is your target audience—or who *are* your target audiences?

- How are viewers likely to come across your website? For example, will most people get to your site via referrals from other clients? By searching for local businesses in your industry? From your heavy investment in Instagram ads?

The next step is deciding what pages you need on your website. You'll need a home page, clearly. What about an "About Us" page to differentiate you from your competition and tell your story? A services page? Product pages? A contact page, a blog section, an employment opportunities page? Don't go overboard—limit the pages to what you truly need but map the content out.

Finally, develop a creative brief for *each page*. Every page of the site should have a purpose and a creative brief will help you get clear on what each page sets out to do. Don't try to write the website all at once; write each page individually so that you can focus on the creative brief for just that page.

A few things to remember as you work:

- Stay focused on what your target audience needs to hear, not what you want to tell them.

- Each page should have some next action to take, otherwise you've led people into a wall. You always want people either taking a key action or interacting more with your brand.

- An "About Us" or "About Me" page isn't really about you— rather use these pages to spell out what you can do for your prospective client or customer.

- Keep your brand voice consistent across all pages.

- Get a proofreader (or at least a second set of eyes) to look over your site before going live. Too many typos make your company or organization seem less professional.

Once you finish your briefs, go ahead and write your copy, and edit, edit, edit. Then you can partner with your web designer to bring the whole site to life.

After the first round of design is done and your copy is in place, come together with your designer (in person or virtually) to work together to tweak and improve.

Case in Point

Understanding the role of your website relative to the role of its pages can get a little confusing. So let's look at a couple of (fictional) examples to make things clearer.

ThriftyTrippy.net is a discount vacation package website.
The overall purpose and goal of the website is to get people to purchase vacation packages. But the goal of the "Our Company" page is to encourage trust in the company; the goal of the "Sweepstakes" page is to get people to sign up for emails; the goal of the "Contact" page is to get the hesitant or confused traveler to get in touch. Only the actual vacation package pages have the goals of getting people to book.

OuttaSite.biz is a web design agency website.
Most visitors will be coming to this site to see if they're interested in hiring the agency so the overall goal of the website is to get people to fill out the contact form. Meanwhile, the goal of the "Case Studies" page is to get people to click and view the agency's impressive work, whereas the goal of the blog section is to get visitors to read the agency's posts and, in the process, get a feel for their expertise.

TheAudaciousAubergine.eat is a restaurant website.
The primary goal is to get people to make reservations and commit to visiting the restaurant. The CTA on the "Menu" pages is to make a reservation but the CTA on the "Special Events" page is

to contact the restaurant to reserve space. And the CTA for the take-out section is to select items and order.

KEEP IN MIND

Writing an entire website is a huge project—but take the process step-by-step, page by page, and message by message and you'll get it written in no time.

Key Takeaways

Your website is a crucial point of contact. Put some serious attention toward writing your site—which will speak for you and your organization when you can't be there yourself.

Consider the visitor's perspective. What kind of information will visitors be looking for when they get to your site? What are they wondering about your organization?

Give them the information they need to take action. Your website should have one overarching purpose, goal, and desired action (or any combination of all three). Make sure you convey the messages that will encourage your visitors to take that action.

Action Items

Write a creative brief for the site as a whole, then one for each page. Your website needs to function well as a whole, but each page also has its own requirements and goals.

Write one page at a time. Don't try to conquer writing the entire site at once. Break the task down page by page and be sure to give yourself time to walk away and come back to each part.

Include a CTA on each page. Give people a chance to get more involved with your brand on every page of your website. You may suggest that people look at your content or get in touch, but every page should give them something to do next.

CHAPTER 20

WRITING FOR DIGITAL AD PLATFORMS

In order to scale significantly, that is, to reach a big audience, most businesses will need to invest in digital ads. To be clear, this chapter is by no means a "how-to" on writing digital ads. Paid media is a complicated and ever-changing landscape. Before you commit money to this endeavor, do some serious research and learning.

What I *can* offer are some best practices and key considerations to use when you're ready to write your digital ads. Again, testing (see chapter 15 page 95), will come into play. Most platforms make testing ad creative ("creative" meaning copy and images) simple so make sure you're putting money behind those testing techniques that perform best.

The first place where most businesses dip their toes into paid media is on the social platforms—Facebook, Instagram, YouTube, Twitter, and the like. But there are platforms that will let you disperse your ad across multiple sites and in multiple placements. I talk a bit about those in this chapter, too.

Strategy Session

Every ad platform is unique. Before you even start planning what you'll write, spend some time on each platform, reading and clicking on the ads you see. Take screenshots of ads you like and then analyze why you think they'd be effective (refer back to chapter 13, page 84). Then apply these questions:

Where does my target audience spend time online? If you're targeting parents of high school students for example, your audience is not likely to be actively using the hottest new app. You want to run ads on the platforms where your target audience is already spending their time. At the time of this book's publishing, the following are the most popular social ad platforms, and they likely will be for a while until competitors can build up enough traction to challenge them.

- **Facebook and Instagram.** Both owned by Facebook, these services have different policies and character counts for their ads.

- **Google Ads.** Google lets you serve up ads as search results, but you can also create both copy-only and image ads to distribute across the Google network.

- **YouTube.** As you might expect, ads on YouTube are all videos, which can be a very compelling way to convey your message.

- **LinkedIn.** This professional networking site is great for targeting people by profession and seems especially valuable for B2B companies (businesses selling to other businesses).

- **Pinterest.** This often-overlooked site is more like a search engine than anything else, and serving up ads to audiences looking for offerings like yours can pair well with the site's actively shopping users.

- **Ad Networks and Content Ad Networks.** These companies allow you to create an ad that gets dispersed across a wide array of websites. Though the audience is broad, you're generally not able to choose which sites your ad displays on. Currently, you can create banner ads, video ads, retargeting ads (reaching people who have been to your site but left), and even content ads that look similar to the content on the website on which you are advertising. Do your research before investing because the minimum spends on these networks can be steep.

What are the ad policies? Facebook, for example, is notorious for having an extensive list of policies for the advertisements it carries and for quickly removing ads that transgress (even accidentally). It's also not averse to shutting an entire ad account down, so be sure your copy and images adhere to the rules—a good practice no matter which ad platform you choose.

What's the maximum character count? You need to know how many letters (and spaces) you can use in your ad. This directive will apply to both the body and headlines (and any other copy areas). Make sure you're clear on this first; you don't want to write up your ads and then have to trim 75 percent of them.

Is your audience looking for ads or are they simply finding them? As you write your ad copy, think carefully about how people are likely to encounter your ad. Google search ads, for example, are displayed when someone performs a search relevant to your ad specifications, meaning the audience is actively looking for information. But Facebook and Instagram ads, which are targeted to your ideal audience, will appear as users are scrolling through their feed or watching stories. How will you write your ad for someone searching for a solution versus for someone engaged in an unrelated task?

Case in Point

Even when you know what you want to say, writing a digital ad can be very difficult—especially with multiple versions. A "swipe file" in this case can come in handy.

"Swipe files" are collections of actual advertisements you've seen out in the wild and grabbed to look at again later. For digital ads, grabbing swipe will likely involve taking screenshots.

Now to be very clear, the purpose of swipe files is *not* to steal copy. That's unethical and, just as important, doesn't work. The copy that's effective for someone else may not be right for your brand. Plus, just because an ad is running doesn't mean the copy works. The company may be testing!

But what swipe files let you do is collect inspiration. You should already be taking the time to notice, read, and analyze the ads being shown to you on these platforms. So grab swipe and save a particularly interesting, unusual, or effective ad that you come across. If you like the way someone started a line of copy, transitioned to another topic, or, really, any aspect, take a screenshot and save the ad.

Now, I would *not* recommend looking at your swipe right before you begin a project. You don't want to be too influenced too soon. Write a few versions of your ad while you're fresh. Then, once you start hitting a creativity wall, dig into your swipe file and see how you can take some of those interesting tactics and make them your own.

Keep adding to your swipe file, and you'll always have inspiration as you write and test new ads.

KEEP IN MIND

Paying for online traffic by investing money in ads that bring people to your site or landing page can be a great way to build your business—if you approach the situation right. Educate yourself as to how to use your platform of choice and then follow these guidelines for writing your ad copy.

Key Takeaways

Research and understand ad platforms before choosing. Every digital advertising platform is different, reaching different people in different ways. Make sure you're clear about exactly why you're choosing a platform before you jump in.

Learn the policies inside and out. Ad platform policies can be complicated and failing to follow them can result in wasted time and money, disapproved ads, or, in the worst-case scenario, a shut down ad account. Familiarize yourself before you even start writing.

Write copy that reflects how readers will interact with the ad. Consider what your audience is likely doing when they encounter your message. Doing so will affect the way you write as well as the messaging you use to catch their attention.

Action Items

Choose one advertising platform to start with. Don't try to create ads on more than one digital ad platform at once. Start with the one you feel is the best place to reach your audience. After you've seen some success, add another.

Start noticing, reading, and analyzing the ads you see. There is no guarantee that every digital ad you come across is successful but for inspiration, take the time to read and evaluate ads you come across.

Write multiple versions to test. Every ad platform makes testing your creative easy, and you should take full advantage. Start by writing multiple versions to test immediately and then create different iterations to test as you continue running your ads.

CHAPTER 21

TIPS FOR WRITING IN ANY MEDIUM

We've dipped our toes into writing emails, email funnels, websites, and social ads, but that's only the beginning. Copy can be found in many mediums. Although I cannot fit how-to advice for writing in each and every medium in these pages, I *can* give you some tips, tools, and tactics for approaching each new project, whatever the medium.

This chapter goes over considerations needed for any type of project in order to learn how to assess the ways the medium you're working in affects your message. Use the copywriting checklist to help you size up your work, no matter which medium you're writing copy for.

Strategy Session

You can't put the same message into each type of project. The message in an email is going to be different from the message in a banner ad. Each format has its own unique needs and constraints. Gear your message to the way your audience experiences your ad—and stay within the medium's constraints—and you've got the keys for crafting effective copy. Here are the steps to follow:

Step #1: Start by considering how much literal space you have for copy. The medium affects the size of the piece, even for digital projects. And that includes the size that your copy can be, and how much copy you can fit into a space.

For example, an email or full-page newspaper ad has a lot of room, so you can have more copy and bigger type. A banner ad on a website has a lot less physical space, so your copy has to be shorter and smaller.

Step #2: Think about where and how people are seeing your copy. If they're viewing a magazine ad, they might be flipping through a fashion magazine or reading a trade journal. Which? Are they seeing your copy in a newspaper or on the side of a bus? In their in-box? What's happening around them while your copy is being presented? How will that affect the way a viewer receives your information?

For example, with a fashion magazine, they could be flipping through it at a hair salon or in their own home, meaning they're looking at the pages relatively quickly and casually. A trade magazine—the term for a magazine that caters specifically to a particular type of business—is very different. Its readers are much more likely to actually look at the ads because they know that they're geared toward their professional interests.

Step #3: Ask yourself, "What are the key points that must be conveyed?" Not the key points anyone would need to know but the most essential points *this* audience needs to know in order to take your desired action.

For example, a brochure for a furniture store and the store's website will have different messaging. Some overlap may occur, but the message should cater to the audience's experience with the medium. With a brochure, the customer has actually been to the store and seen the furniture in person. This situation should result in a different message than the website, whose readers may not have visited the showroom.

Step #4: Evaluate the project's limits as you outline. It sounds a little crazy, perhaps, but limitations actually make writing easier. You're already "limited," in a way, by knowing what you have to get across to the reader. You need to convey the benefit, have a strong CTA, and write within the brand voice. Now add in the limits of your medium, and your blank page becomes a much smaller box for you to fill in.

Step #5: Revise your copy before sending to the designer *and* revise again when in layout. Copy can look very different when laid out in a design than when in your copy doc. You may find you need to trim even more to keep the piece readable.

Case in Point

Even the most seasoned copywriters can benefit from going back to basics and reviewing the fundamental copywriting principles periodically. On the next page is a checklist designed to help you focus before you begin writing and to guide your edits and revisions after you finish each draft. Use this tool for any kind of copy you're working on.

Don't try to speed through the list—really take some time to answer each question and objectively evaluate your copywriting. With that in mind.

YOUR COPYWRITING CHECKLIST

☐ Have you led with the benefit?

☐ Have you explored how this benefit can transform the reader or their lives?

☐ Do you support the benefit with features?

☐ Is your copy easy to scan and the main message clear?

☐ Did you keep your lines and sentences short?

☐ Does the call to action make clear what the reader will experience next if they take the action?

☐ Have you been concise and purposeful?

☐ Have you used words and phrases that will resonate with your target audience?

☐ Have you used words and phrases within the brand voice?

☐ Is your brand voice consistent throughout the piece?

☐ Is the reader's next step clear? Does taking that step feel compelling and irresistible?

☐ Did you write a clear and direct call to action?

☐ Will your copy fit within the constraints of the medium?

☐ Are the messages you want to convey presented in an order that makes sense?

☐ Are there any words, phrases, or messages that are unnecessary in this piece?

KEEP IN MIND

You'll use copy in a multitude of ways and in a multitude of places throughout your career. Here are a few tips for ensuring that you're putting out your best work, no matter the medium.

Key Takeaways

All copy should follow the foundational principles you've learned. One of the most common pitfalls for new copywriters is to get so excited with what they're working on that they forget to use the basic principles of copy. I call these concepts foundational for a reason: They're what *all* of your copy should be built on.

The medium will dictate how much copy you can use. Your message is going to have to change depending on the venue and on how much space you have to use. Consider these constraints before you start writing.

Consider how readers will encounter the copy. Where are they likely to come across this particular copy and at what point in the customer journey? Both of these factors should strongly impact the copy you write.

Action Items

Define the piece and the goals. Start out by getting clear on exactly what you're writing and what your desired outcome is, specifically for this copywriting project. Don't confuse this with your overall business goals!

Identify how the medium limits you. Constraints can be a challenge but they can also help you refine your messaging down to the most crucial points needed to convey.

Write—and refine—using your checklist. Use the provided checklist to stay focused as you plan your copy, write your copy, and then edit your copy.

CHAPTER 22

HOW TO HIRE A COPYWRITER WHEN YOUR BUSINESS GROWS

I wrote this book because I believe everyone—and especially business owners—can benefit from having copywriting skills. I hope you put everything you've learned in this book to good use on a regular basis.

However, part of the goal of any business is growth. And part of growth is outsourcing to experts when you're able. Because your message is such a crucial part of your success, hiring an expert to take on some of your highest-impact copywriting work makes sense.

But not all copywriters are equal. And, buyer beware, not all people who call themselves copywriters actually are. So this final chapter is designed to help you find the best copywriter for you and your projects and to work with them well.

Strategy Session

Once you put out the call for a copywriter—to your contacts, in Facebook groups, even in job postings—you're likely to get a flood of responses. Plenty of people *want* to be copywriters but far fewer will meet the standard. Let's start this discussion by talking about what to look for and what to avoid. (Would-be copywriters, take note! Can you measure up?)

THREE ASPECTS TO LOOK FOR IN A COPYWRITER

They must have a website with a portfolio. This requirement is non-negotiable. A copywriter needs to have their previous work available for you to evaluate.

They must have breadth and depth of experience. The portfolio should demonstrate that this copywriter is able to write in different voices and for different mediums. If so, they'll be able to hit the ground running with *your* brand voice and projects.

Their site should be focused on you and your needs. This prospective hire's website should demonstrate effective copywriting. The site should be about what *you* will get out of working with them (the benefit to the consumer!). If they can't effectively market themselves, how can they deliver your message?

THREE RED FLAGS

Their site presents content only. If a potential copywriter's online portfolio is full of content (blog posts, articles, etc.), run. Far and fast. They're not a copywriter, they're a content writer—and what's worse, they don't know the difference.

Their copy is long and meandering. As you know, copywriting is about honing a message down to the essential elements. If they can't pare down for themselves on their own website, how will they do so for you?

Their professional social profiles are, well, unprofessional. Looking at the social profiles (LinkedIn, Facebook, Instagram) of a prospective copywriter is always worth the effort. Someone who has a great website but posts messages on social media like "Ugh, clients are so annoying!" lacks an adequate level of professionalism.

WHEN YOU FIND A GOOD CANDIDATE

After you make contact, a good copywriter will schedule an intro or discovery call with you to ask questions about your company and the project and get a good handle on all the project will entail. They won't (and shouldn't!) give you rates until they discuss the project with you because every project and client have their own needs. Soon after the call, they should send you a detailed description of the project (per your call), the date you agreed on for receiving the first round of copy, and their price.

NEED FOR A COPYWRITING CERTIFICATION?

You do not need to look for a copywriting certification. This document only proves one thing: They paid for a course. With copywriting, the proof is in the pudding. Look for a great portfolio that showcases excellent work.

AFTER THE HIRE

After you hire a copywriter, they'll schedule an input or kick-off call to dig into the details of the project, your business objectives, your brand voice, your target audience. A good copywriter will prompt you to think about things you haven't even considered yet! Your copywriter will use this information in their creative brief to guide them as they write. They may or may not send you further questions as they go.

After they finish the first round of copy, the copywriter will review what they've written with you. Expect to have feedback—it's a standard part of the process; you have expertise in your head that your copywriter couldn't know to ask about and that you couldn't know to offer.

When you share your feedback, certainly call out what you like. But with what doesn't work, be sure to let the copywriter know *why* the copy is not working. Your copywriter needs this input to refine and improve. Don't try to rewrite anything—you hired a copywriter for a reason! Expect to give a round or two of feedback to polish the copy and get the project to a place where you're delighted.

Case in Point

You can look at a copywriter's portfolio a hundred times but how can you be confident they'll be able to write well for *you*?

Of course, you can never be 100 percent sure. But a tactic that can help you inch a bit closer to certainty is a copy test.

A copy test is a *short* assignment that you ask your top two or three candidates to write for you. Note the emphasis on the word "short"—this should be something a copywriter could finish in under a half hour.

Be sure this is *not* work you're going to use if you don't hire them. A copy test is not a method for scamming free work from well-meaning applicants. Historically, copy tests are unpaid work (part of why the tests should be short). But there's been a steadily growing trend to pay for copy tests, and I'd encourage you to consider doing so. Paying for a half-hour's worth of time to two or three candidates to find the right copywriter for you is well worth the investment.

So what could you do for your copy test? Obviously, the test can (and arguably should) be informed by your actual copy project needs. Here are a few ideas:

Subject lines. Send your candidates one of your marketing emails and ask them to come up with three subject line options.

Headlines. Give your candidates access to one of your webpages or landing pages and ask them how they'd rewrite the headline or the headline and subhead.

Bio. Ask your candidates to rewrite your current (short!) biography.

What to look for in the test results:

- Did the copywriter ask additional questions? Questions are good because they show that the writer wants to understand you and the project as much as possible.

- Does the brand voice match yours?

- Does the copy adhere to the principles you've learned in this book?

- Did the copywriter follow directions?

- Did the copywriter go above and beyond? Though going above and beyond is not essential, if you ask for three subject lines and they give you five, or if you ask them to rewrite the headline and they rewrite the head, subhead, and first paragraph of body copy, you can bet they care about the work.

Choosing the right copywriter can have a major impact on your business. Evaluate your options carefully and make sure you're working with a pro.

Key Takeaways

Look at a prospective copywriter's portfolio. Read through their website to make sure they're capable of writing in different brand voices and for different types of projects. Doing so helps ensure they'll be able to hit the ground running with you.

Look for someone who takes the work off your plate. A true professional should make your life easier. They should set expectations, check in, and follow up.

Expect a few rounds of feedback to refine the work. Only very rarely will a copywriter get it all *exactly* right immediately. Embrace the feedback cycles to collaborate and make the work as excellent as possible.

Action Items

Put out the call. When you need a copywriter, tell your contacts, post in Facebook groups, post job listings—the wider you cast your net, the more responses you'll get. Plenty of the responses won't be worth your time, but you can use the info in this chapter to quickly weed out the ones who won't work.

Refine your list through portfolio reviews and discovery calls. Narrow down your roster of applicants by first reviewing their websites and portfolios, and second, by scheduling discovery calls (info calls) with your top three to five candidates.

Consider a copy test. When you've narrowed down your list to two or three copywriters, consider giving each a short copy test to get a better feel for who will write best in your brand voice and for your projects. Be willing to pay for the work in order to find the best fit.

A Few Last Notes

Phew! We've come to the end of the book and you've taken in a ton of information, probably in a pretty short period of time. Good for you!

Here's something I want you to remember as you put all that information to use: Mastering all of these skills is going to take plenty of practice. As adults, we often forget what it's like to learn something new and be challenged by putting a new skill into action. We think, "Okay, sure, I get that I'm brand new to this," but we still tend to become frustrated that we're not immediately proficient at what we try.

Remember that copywriting is an entire career! Be kind to yourself if (when) you don't nail each and every piece of copy immediately. If you're a business owner, you're already so far ahead of the competition just by knowing what you now know. And if you want to be a professional copywriter, you've taken a significant first step toward success.

Very likely, there will be times in your copywriting journey when you get frustrated or doubt your abilities. All completely normal. (In fact, I'd be concerned if you *didn't*!) If so, first be kind to yourself, and second, come back to what your messages are really about: connecting with a target audience who wants the solution you have for them.

Keep your focus on that *true* purpose for your copywriting and you'll always be heading in the right direction.

Keep writing, keep editing, and keep getting your messages out there.

Resources

Podcasts

Build Your Copywriting Business—I'm biased, of course, because this is my podcast, but we work hard to pack each episode full of useful information and insightful guests.

Online Marketing Made Easy—Amy Porterfield does a great job of demystifying digital marketing concepts and tactics, making them accessible for people at any level of business.

Marketing School—This podcast serves up about five minutes of daily marketing and business advice and, despite its grueling publishing schedule, rarely disappoints.

Foot Traffic Podcast—Catering to both digital and brick-and-mortar businesses, this podcast delivers strategy and insight about marketing, business systems, scaling, and more.

Websites

FilthyRichWriter.com—Again, I'm slightly biased, but with more than 500 articles, we've worked hard to make each post as actionable as possible. Worth a look.

DigitalMarketer.com—One of the most trusted and followed marketing sites on the internet, it's always up on the latest trends and news.

Hubspot.com—HubSpot itself is a software, but the site's blog is chock full of useful information for marketers and business owners.

ContentMarketingInstitute.com—For help with the content (and content strategy) side of your business, this organization's blog has ideas and action items galore.

Books

Influence **by Robert Cialdini**—This book is a must-read that offers tons of insight into human behavior and (ethical) marketing tactics.

Building a Story Brand **by Donald Miller**—Now that you know the principles of copywriting, you're not going to find a lot that's new here, but Miller has a great way of framing concepts that might further help you implement them.

Design Basics Index **by Jim Krause**—You do NOT need to know design to write copy . . . but a basic understanding will never hurt. This book offers just the right level of design education.

Brand Thinking and Other Noble Pursuits **by Debbie Millman**—This book digs into why and how we create brands and offers up plenty of ideas for developing and writing for your own business (or for your clients!).

References

Anderson, Tom. "What's the Secret behind Nike's 'Just Do It' Campaign?" *Blinkist Magazine*, August 23, 2019. Blinkist.com/magazine/posts/emotional-branding-secret -behind-nikes-just-campaign.

Bell, Jonathan. "Thinking Small: Tracing Volkswagen's Rebellious Streak." *Wallpaper**, November 7, 2016. Wallpaper.com /lifestyle/how-volkswagen-changed-advertising-ugly -is-only-skin-deep.

Cramer-Flood, Ethan. "Worldwide Digital Ad Spending 2021." eMarketer, April 29, 2021. eMarketer.com/content/worldwide -digital-ad-spending-2021.

Daddona, Matthew. "Got Milk? How the Iconic Campaign Came to Be, 25 Years Ago." *Fast Company*, June 13, 2018. FastCompany .com/40556502/got-milk-how-the-iconic-campaign-came-to -be-25-years-ago.

Facebook. "Facebook Unveils Facebook Ads." November 6, 2007. eabout.FB.com/news/2007/11/facebook-unveils-facebook-ads.

Fowler, Glen. "John Caples, 90, Author in 1926 of 'They Laughed When . . .' Ad." *New York Times*, June 11, 1990. NYTimes.com /1990/06/11/obituaries/john-caples-90-author-in-1926-of -they-laughed-when-ad.html.

Kemp, Simon. "Digital 2021: The Latest Insights into the 'State of Digital.'" We Are Social, January 27, 2021. WeAreSocial.com/uk /blog/2021/01/digital-2021-the-latest-insights-into-the-state -of-digital.

Index

E

Editing process, 32–33, 61, 80–83
Email
  copy, 17
  formatting example, 77
  funnels, 112–115, 117
  letter-style, 108, 109–111
  promotional, 107, 109–111
  subject line dos and
    don'ts, 108, 111
  supplements company
    case study, 115–116
Evaluating copy, 86, 88

F

Facebook ads, 6, 14, 123
Formatting copy docs, 74–79

G

Getting started tips, 23–24
GoDaddy brand voice, 105
Google Ads, 123
"Got Milk?" tagline, 6

H

Headlines, 65, 68
Hiring copywriters, 132–137
Hooks, creating effective, 54–58

I

Instagram ads, 14, 123
Internet, 11–14

J

"Just Do It" tagline, 6

K

Kate Spade brand voice, 105

L

Language choice, 29–30
LinkedIn ads, 123

M

Messaging, importance of, 3
Multivariate testing, 96–97

N

Narrative approach to
  hooks, 55–56
Nike tagline, 6
Noticing copy, 85, 87–88

O

Open rate, 15, 90
Opt-in copy, 19–20

P

Paragraphs, 65, 68
Pinterest ads, 123
Planning strategy, 26
Postcard formatting
  example, 77–78
Product description
  copy, 20–21, 47–52
Purpose, determining, 26

R

Readability of copy, 64–68
Rewriting copy, 86–87, 88
Rules of copywriting, 25–33

S

Search engine optimization
  (SEO) copy, 21–22
Sentences, 65, 68
Social ad copy, 18–19
Social media
  advertising platforms, 122–126
  captions, 22–23
  copywriting impacts of, 13–14
Structuring copy, 64–68
Subheads, 65, 68
Surveys, use of, 37–39, 40
Swipe files, 125

Acknowledgments

This book wouldn't have been possible without the support from our team at Nicki K Media. Thank you Kate, Kaitlyn, Julie, Tracy, and Meaghan—I'm constantly marveling at how lucky our company is to have you.

Thank you to Stuart, Dori, Shannon, Ashley, Stacy, Abigail, and all of our other copy coaches (past and future!) for helping guide our copywriting students. You guys are dynamos and I'm so thrilled for your successes.

Thank you, too, to our Filthy Rich Writer and Comprehensive Copywriting Academy community. Your dedication, hard work, and passion inspire me, and it is a true joy and honor to be part of your professional journeys.

I have so much gratitude for the brilliant creative directors and designers who've taught me so much throughout my career, especially my best friend, Melody, who was my first true design *partner*.

And, finally, thank you again to my parents, Mike and Pam, and my brother, Jeff, for loving me and believing in me. Who knew that a crazy little idea for a copywriting course would turn into all of this?

About the Author

 **Nicki Krawczyk** is a copywriter with 15-plus years' experience writing for businesses small and large, including Hasbro, adidas, Tripadvisor, T.J.Maxx, and Keurig. She cohosts the popular *Build Your Copywriting Business* podcast.

She also coaches novice copywriters to build thriving careers through her website, FilthyRichWriter.com, and her Comprehensive Copywriting Academy. For Nicki, being "filthy rich" means having a job you love, being good at what you do, and making great money doing it.